www.AllysonE

WHAT OTHERS ARE SAYING ABOUT ALLYSON AND THIS BOOK

"Misunderstood is a revelation of authentic personal growth. Allyson exposes her behaviors and thoughts with deep vulnerability, offering her processes for achieving acceptance and serenity. As a therapist and life coach, she not only presents skills and strategies but welcomes you to witness personal application to her thoughts and behaviors. Honest, humble, and truly human, Allyson lives what she teaches."

~ JoAnn W. Payne, LCSW

"Allyson speaks to her readers from the most truthful place an author can write: unapologetic vulnerability. Sharing her personal growth throughout her life, admitting that she's a work in progress (as we all are until we take our last breath), and practicing her own techniques before recommending them to her readers, are just a few ways she exemplifies honest commitment to the success of others. Misunderstood is well-written, informative, honest, and challenges the reader to put himself or herself under the microscope and try a different approach to being emotionally grounded and communicative. Complete with worksheets for practical implementation, this book will be highly beneficial to all who read it."

~ Don Metcalf

"I have found Allyson to be wise, caring, thoughtful, and openhearted. She has the ability to gently give me feedback that makes me stop and think in a whole new way, benefiting each and every relationship in my life. I found the experience led me to a whole new level. – Wow – What a gift! My experience has been amazing! I found the program to be life-changing! What a wonderful journey of self-awareness, self-discovery, and developing life skills to become a better me. I was inspired and challenged!"

~ Tina Bernheimer

"Allyson has taught me how to love myself, along with believing in myself and my dreams. There honestly aren't enough words to say how lucky I am to have her in my life as Coach, a Therapist, and honestly, a friend. All I can really say is she's an amazing person. Thank you, Allyson, for all you have helped me with."

~ Tim Ramey

"Allyson, and the work she does, has changed my life. I went from being very angry and blaming to taking responsibility for my life. The journey, at times, was hard and painful, but well worth it. The knowledge and tools I've learned are invaluable. I believe in the work Allyson is doing."

~ Debbie Hellmann

"Is there any part of you that feels misunderstood? That is a question I vividly remember Allyson asking me during our first session together. Rarely did I feel seen, heard, or understood, which lead to a lot of unresolved anger, resentment, and disappointment. I had developed patterns of communicating and behaving that were ineffective. These same patterns began defining my life and relationships as an adult. With Allyson's guidance and support, I've rid myself of my sharp exterior. My energy has completely shifted, and I am more open, honest, and authentic than I thought possible. I've learned how to self-reflect, practice self-awareness, and ultimately, better understand how my deepest needs drive the way I behave and make decisions. I give myself permission to feel without judgment and practice self-compassion when I make mistakes. Most importantly, I feel confident that I have the foundation and tools necessary to redirect myself, should I find myself off track. My life has been transformed by this work, and thanks to Allyson, I am a better daughter, aunt, sibling, friend, and human being because of it."

~ Kelly Klein

"When I think of Allyson, the word unstoppable comes to mind. She has taken what life has thrown at her and turned those lessons into opportunities for growth—both for herself and those around her. You'll find she has an uncanny way of getting to the root of the issue and speaking to the heart of the person. After a year of working with Allyson, I can feel a change in myself. I am developing confidence I knew was there but didn't know how to bring to the surface. I also now have tools that I didn't have before to help myself and my family. Watching Allyson grow has inspired me to step out and look for new and creative ways to develop."

~ Brittany Czirr

www.AllysonBlythe.com

Rewriting The Rules of Dignity & Self-Respect!

www.AllysonBlythe.com

www.AllysonBlythe.com

MISUNDERSTOOD

By

Allyson Blythe

TRANSFORM
PUBLISHING

www.AllysonBlythe.com

Misunderstood

Rewriting The Rules of Dignity and Self-Respect

Published by:
Transform Publishing
www.TransformPublish.com

Address all inquiries to:
Allyson Blythe
859-341-7773
AllysonBlythe@live.com
www.AllysonBlythe.com

ISBN: 978-1-0878-8666-4
LOC: 2020939614
Senior Editor: Elena Rahrig
Editor: Lasina Jensen
Cover Design: Elena Rahrig
Interior Book Layout: Elena Rahrig

Every attempt has been made to properly source all quotes.

Printed in the United States of America
First Edition

www.AllysonBlythe.com

Dedication

To My Daughter

For the person you are and all that you'll become. You are the reason for much of my work and the inspiration of my life lessons and learning. You are a gift, and I am forever grateful for the chance to be your mom. I hope to make you proud and show you all the things I didn't know before, so you show up strong, true, and fully believing in your amazing self!

To My Younger Self

This is for the person you tried to be, the wars you fought, and the lessons you endured. I see the effort you put into people, relationships, and life in general. Thank you for that scrappy, feisty little spirit you've always had; I know how hard you tried. I honor and celebrate every misguided effort you put forth. You carried the load for a long time, and I assure you, I've got it now. You can rest easy, and I'll take it from here.

www.AllysonBlythe.com

Acknowledgment

Thank you to my clients who are my inspiration and purpose in much of the work I do. I believe, together, we can make the world a better place through connection and community. Thanks for being on this journey with me and challenging me to always just stay one page ahead.

Thank you to the women in my family who came before me. Lifelong legacies are being laid to rest in this work. I thank you for the road you traveled and the teachings you offered me. We come from a long line of good hearts, few resources, and trying too damn hard. This is the permission I wish you had been granted long ago. The world deserves our best boundaried selves!

Thank you to Cindy, for always having a listening ear, a proud spirit, and the right words to say. You've walked with me on this long and winding path, never leaving my side. You've gone above and beyond and deserve a gold medal in the friendship category!

A huge thank you to Mike for supporting me in every facet imaginable. You are my biggest cheerleader, my greatest supporter, and strongest sounding board. You helped me to believe in myself and to know this work was truly possible. You have been a powerful test ground and launching pad for my own S.O.S. work.

www.AllysonBlythe.com

To everyone who has contributed to the depths of this work. I may not have seen it at the time, nor understood, how much I needed your contribution, but wow, thank you! Thank you for what you've taught me and the ways you've offered tough learning and good practice. Sorry for the damage I may have done in the process. No one said I was an easy learner!

~ Allyson Blythe

Contents

Preface

From the time I was a little girl, I knew there was a greater mission I was called to fulfill. It was never a question; I was destined for the helping field. I am a master at this emotional stuff for other people. I can sit with them and immediately sense their struggles and have been coined as a Coach and Therapist who *just gets it.* I am a champ at celebrating the smallest of wins and a trooper for sitting with the deepest imaginable pain and devastation. The public face is an easy one to wear. Yet, what most people would never have guessed is, the greatest pain and confusion I carried was my own.

When I share any of my own struggles and defects with my clients, the question I always hear is a shocked *"You?" "Yes, me."* is my strong affirmative answer. Despite the letters behind my name, the degrees that hang on the wall, the years of experience, and the power of a tenacious, determined heart, yes, the struggle is incredibly real. I most definitely have not been immune to the childhood conditioning of *being good.*

Of course, I've grappled with life and had only the tools, insight, and resources of the imperfect generations before me. I wasn't born with a manual or a script to follow. Though perhaps a master at managing and offering insight about your pain behind closed doors, I couldn't seem to guide nor direct my way through my own personal pain.

Misunderstood is my personal contribution, an offering for all those wishing there is a life manual to guide, direct, and inspire. May you find the hope, encouragement, and inspiration in this personal script.

Foreword

As a Publisher, I regularly receive hundreds of manuscripts; therefore, I cannot possibly accommodate them all. When I saw this book, Misunderstood, laying amidst the pile, the title captivated my attention. As a person who has a need to be heard and understood, I knew this book would be a masterpiece. The more I read of the manuscript, the more my eyes were opened to the overall profound and invigorating content.

In this book, Allyson reveals her vulnerability surrounding the ways in which she was misunderstood, and how she misunderstood others. Moreover, she gives readers the S.O.S. Toolbox with ten power[ful] tools that are easy to understand and implement.

Allyson states, "There was a time when I was losing my grip and the ground beneath me seemed to be crumbling. My head felt like someone had stuck it into a blender and my heart pounded with formidable betrayal. At the time, I wished I had a life manual to guide, direct, and inspire me. Through my own life experiences and wisdom learned, I was now able to write the life manual for others in this book, Misunderstood."

Allyson's statement, along with her credentials, are only two reasons why I knew this book would offer tremendous value. Allyson's knowledge and wisdom, experience, and her S.O.S. Toolbox, which are shared in this book, are much needed by everyone.

As more people are stepping up to become Authors, the more self-help books flood the market. Many self-help books include, or lead to, some sort of model to follow. I must say, we see models (all the time) that are not effective. Many are out of sequence; meaning, you truly should complete later steps first, and first steps later. We also witness models that simply lack steps that must be taken to make the entire model effective. So, when Allyson's model showed up on my desk, it was a breath of fresh air.

Finally, someone with enough knowledge and wisdom to not *fake it, until she makes it*. Finally, someone who spent the time needed (over twenty-five years, in fact) to create a life manual that leads to understanding and healthy relationships maintained by boundaries. Finally, someone who not only lives her model but tested it time and again to prove it is life changing.

As I read through this book, I could not help but live out each step in each chapter. That's right, me, the Publisher, has already applied Allyson's teachings. Let me warn you, they work!

Throughout this book, Allyson uses great examples and visuals to drive her points home. I especially love her story about how she "lost her shit over a banana."

www.AllysonBlythe.com

Throughout this book, Allyson is transparent, allowing her readers to truly connect with her through circumstances. She truly is raw, real, and relatable to all who take time to learn from her.

So, if you face challenges in life, have a difficult time being misunderstood, are consistently overlooked and walked on, and are unclear about how to live your best life now, this book, Misunderstood, is your #1 guide currently on the market.

Lastly, I want to personally say, "Thank You" to Allyson Blythe for opening her heart to her readers. She has shared personal details, that most would be uncomfortable doing. It takes a lot of courage to create what she has created; and in the name of love, she has proven she truly cares about others. Anyone who reads this book, completes the exercises, and applies the wisdom, will no longer be *misunderstood*. Here at Transform Publishing, we look forward to assisting Allyson with all her future books.

Elena Rahrig
Founding CEO of Transform Publishing
567-259-6454
www.TransformPublish.com
Info@ETransformInternational.com

www.AllysonBlythe.com

Introduction

"When you choose to forgive the same people over and over again you do so because you don't want to believe your time loving them was wasted. Bad relationships, over time, can become investments that are hard to let go of. The key to freedom is to realize that love is never wasted. The only thing wasted in life is the time you spend focusing on an unhappy situation that will never change to fit your needs, and not realizing the true investment of time and love are the lessons God wanted you to learn."

~ Shannon L. Alder

"This above all: to thine own self be true."

~ William Shakespeare

What if I told you, you are your ultimate problem and brightest solution in every way? What if every blurry-eyed morning, the issue and the answer are in the mirror staring right back at you? What if I told you that you hold the power to create your very best life, and the process can begin right now?

So, I'll ask you:

Are you unhappy?	*Yes*	*No*
Do you feel mistreated?	*Yes*	*No*
Do you tend to work really hard in relationships?	*Yes*	*No*
Are you exhausted? Depleted?	*Yes*	*No*
Do you feel unappreciated?	*Yes*	*No*
Are you overwhelmed?	*Yes*	*No*
Are you unhealthy?	*Yes*	*No*
Are you wandering around broke?	*Yes*	*No*
Are you in relationships in which you are disrespected?	*Yes*	*No*
Are you overworked? Underpaid?	*Yes*	*No*

If you answered *yes* to one or more of the above questions, we need to talk. If you recognize these feelings or find yourself in a chronic state of any of them, it's time to ask yourself, *what is it that I'm allowing?*

According to Dictionary.com, the word *allow* means:

- *to give permission to or for; permit: to allow a student to be absent; No swimming allowed.*
- *to let have; give as one's share; grant as one's right: to allow a person $100 for expenses.*
- *to permit by neglect, oversight, or the like: to allow a door to remain open.*

- *to admit; acknowledge; concede: to allow a claim.*
- *to take into consideration, as by adding or subtracting; set apart: to allow an hour for changing trains.*
- *to permit something to happen or to exist; admit.*

The hard truth is, none of these conditions can exist for long periods of time without your permission. If you are in situations or relationships in which negative feelings are your result, there is something happening that you are co-signing, something that you're allowing. These long-term states don't happen by accident; they require your compliance.

Welcome to Misunderstood, a journey inward in which you will look at what you are allowing in your life. This book is the manual I wish the generations before me and I had been born with. It is the offering of wisdom, insight, and tools to help you take full responsibility for your life. Misunderstood is an inner journey of self-discovery, honesty, and personal accountability to shine light into the deepest corners of your feelings, thoughts, beliefs, needs, habits, and patterns. We will explore the ways you've been misinformed, confused, selling yourself out, settling, working too hard, and working against yourself. Then, you'll be offered the tools, script, and resources to choose differently.

This journey is not one for the faint of heart. Awareness can be a double-edged sword. In fact, some have cautioned that this work should come with a warning label because once you venture in, you can't unlearn or unsee all you discover. Acceptance is part of wisdom, the journey. It's about understanding that you don't always get what you want in life, but as Mick Jagger so wisely offers, "If you try sometimes, you'll find you get what you need."

Chapter 1

Accommodating

"Her feelings she hides.
Her dreams she can't find.
She's losing her mind.
She's falling behind.
She can't find her place.
She's losing her faith.
She's falling from grace.
She's all over the place..."
~ Avril Lavigne, Ben Moody, & Don Gilmore

I lost my shit over a banana. Yup, it was a banana that brought me to the brink of insanity. The headlines read, 'Woman Flies Into A Rage Over The Last Banana.' At least that's how the headline scrolled through my mind.

I was losing my grip and the ground beneath me seemed to be crumbling. My head was scrambled, as though someone had stuck it in a blender and pressed the highest pulse setting. My heart pounded with formidable betrayal from *that woman*... yes, *that woman* eating the last banana that once hung on the wrought iron fruit tree atop the white marble counter. Who would have guessed I could come to the brink and feel capable of grave physical harm *over a banana?*

It was the summer of 2013, while on a girls' trip in Panama City, Florida when my world began to unravel. Just like every other trip we ventured on, I spent most of my time, painstakingly planning and managing our activities and menu. Each of us had our own ideas of fun and adventure, so planning wasn't easy, as it felt important to be sure everyone was happy, content, and well-cared for. Limited to one car, and yet recognizing the different excursions each person desired, the pressure was on to accommodate and please everyone.

Nearing the end of the trip, I was conscious of the limited amount of food that was left and all the activities that hadn't yet unfolded. So, with my mind occupied and energy consumed with the needs of others, imagine my surprise when one of the weekend travelers stumbled out of bed after 10:00 a.m. and grabbed the last banana, without giving a single thought to anyone else in the house.

The walls seemed to cave and the roof shook as she caught the death grip of my eyeballs. Wandering out of the room, she shrugged and said, "What? I'm hungry!"

Oh, hell no... What the hell was happening? Why was I murderously rageful over a banana?

Chapter 2

Caring

"He dreamed of deserts and great empty cities and imagined he could feel the minutes and hours of his life running through him, as though he were nothing but an hourglass of flesh and bone."
~ Laini Taylor, Strange the Dreamer

Painted nails, hair just right, make-up drawn on perfectly, right shoe, left shoe, grab my purse and keys, and head for the door. It was time to go! I had delayed as-long-as I possibly could because many were relying on me. Somehow, I was elected the Social Director; a position I was naturally good at but never sought.

There were seven unread messages on my phone, with four missed calls, and two voicemails. As much as I wanted to attend and be a part of something, I couldn't plaster on the smile, nor muster the enthusiastic energy, for managing the seating arrangements for all the attendees.

In the past, being needed and having the responsibility to make the world go around, made me feel valued, important, and a part of a larger whole. However, something new was brewing inside of me... emotions I couldn't rationalize, nor contain. Something was certainly shifting, pieces deep inside of me were beginning to break loose. I looked upon my life with depletion, disappointment, hostility, and resentment. Once again, my mind was in the blender with thoughts unable to be sorted.

The pain I felt was not a physical sickness, rather a visceral, emotional torment that plagued my spirit. Wadded into a colossal tangled mess, the only emotions I could decipher were annoyance, irritation, depletion, and exhaustion. Like the pain of a raw, sensitive sunburn, I was tender, hypervigilant, and overly conscious in every interaction, fearing the intensity of the searing emotional pain.

Pointblank... I was tired, but not the kind of tired from too many late nights or too much activity. Instead, it was a bone-weary, no energy, can't even see straight kind of tired. The places I used to go were suddenly disappointing, and the things I used to do became increasingly overwhelming. Perhaps most difficult to swallow was the painful realization that the people I had invested heavily in, didn't seem to invest quite so heavily in me. I was tired of showing up. How could this be happening?

Most of my days were spent *peopling*. I made myself readily available, was accommodating, and responded to the immediacy of others' needs. I was consistent and reliable, even when I didn't want to be. If you were in my tribe, I was committed to showing up in every capacity and my circle was ever expanding without much discretion. I had a strong *we* mentality that I thought was the most considerate way to function in the world. I tried anticipating people's needs, was thoughtful and overly conscious of making sure everyone felt comfortable, content, and welcome.

I'm a therapist, of course I understand the human needs of inclusion and belonging. Perhaps, far more conscious of those needs in others than in myself. I also knew all about boundaries. I had read the books, studied a few courses, and certainly recognized the lack in others. Yet, this was about inclusion, fun, and belonging, not boundaries... or so I thought.

Relationships mattered to me. I invested heavily in them and was mindful to go the extra mile. Being deliberate about time spent, while building a sense of community and connection, was essential and drove most of what I did. I managed the tasks of get-togethers with invites, hosting, and details, all the way down to remembering the clean hand towels neatly placed.

When others were struggling, I remembered the details with calls and check-ins, being sure to send good vibes and prayers. It didn't matter if it was a birthday, anniversary, surgery, or a simple cough, I remembered and took action. I was overboard with intent to let them know they mattered. That was kindness, right?

Although I've faced some serious shit in my life, there was always a crew of people, places, and things that gave me the illusion of being connected, loved, and valued. As the crew manager, driver of the ship, social butterfly, and event planner, there was always more than enough activity; yet I always seemed to be the initiator. The frenzy of it all and the quantity of relationships drove me; however, I never stopped to assess and pay attention to the *quality* of any of it. I simply drove relationships and connections. I was fueled by busyness and the chaos of it all.

These were behaviors that served me and others quite well... until suddenly, they didn't. I was not conscious of the price I was paying, nor the toll it was taking on my spirit. How was it that the roles I had played, the tasks I had managed, and the things I had done were suddenly too much, too overwhelming? What was this wild irritability that was rising up within me? For someone who claimed to value kindness so deeply, why was I suddenly feeling incredibly unkind?

New emotions seemed to be fiercely piercing through my veins: irritability, despondence, overwhelm, and chronic disappointment. Everything seemed exceedingly emotionally charged. Social gatherings made me feel annoyed and highly sensitive. Every comment, look, and slight action became a personal attack. I lived in a state of hurt feelings.

The firm grip I always had on life was slipping from my

hands and I simply didn't have the strength to clutch for it anymore. I was exhausted from driving the ship while others simply enjoyed the ride. I was weary from meeting others' needs, with little to no initiation and consideration. Why was I the only one inviting, connecting, and reaching out? I was getting my ass kicked in this invisible emotional battle.

Can you relate? Have you been there? Below is an exercise that will help bring you clarity.

The following apply to me:	
Other people matter greatly to me.	
I put other people ahead of myself.	
I am readily available to others.	
I am highly considerate.	
I anticipate people's needs.	
I am accommodating.	
I want people to be happy.	
I want everyone to feel included.	
I am the initiator in most relationships.	
Community and connection matter to me.	
I remember details about other people's struggles.	
I check in with others to make sure they are doing well.	

The following apply to me:	
I'd like to matter more to people.	
I want to be included.	
I'd like to be considered more.	
I want to be accepted.	
It would be nice if other people are as intentional as I am.	
Community and connection are essential in my life.	
I would like it if people paid more attention to details and knew more about my life.	
I wish others would invite and initiate contact with me.	

What patterns do you see? As you examine your lists, do you see how you relate and function in relationships? Are you giving away what you actually need for yourself? Are you hoping people show up like you do in relationships?

When I started to investigate, assess, and determine what the hell was happening, my eyes started to open to my own martyred, depleted functioning. Yet the ache prevailed; and still, I needed help from a good, reliable friend.

I am sure you have met my friend; in fact, she is probably a friend of yours, too. She can be sneaky and invasive with her habits of random listening and rude invasion of conversations. However, she is handy and smart, too. Her name is Siri. I don't know about your feelings towards her, but our relationship is one of love and hate.

Consumed by my thoughts on a warm, thick fall day, I rewound and reviewed the past years. The decisions made, roles played, behaviors tolerated, words swallowed, relationships managed, and conversations never to be had, all of these made me feel as though I just might drown in the whirling abyss of contemplations, deliberations, and emotions. Managing everything for everyone was what I had always done; so, why now was I exhausted from it all?

I needed answers to gain understanding. So, I asked our good friend, "Siri, what's an existential crisis?"

Here's how she responded:

> *Feelings of loneliness and insignificance in the face of nature are common in an existential crisis. An existential crisis is a moment at which an individual questions if their life has meaning, purpose, or value. It may be commonly, but not necessarily, tied to depression or inevitably negative speculations on purpose in life (e.g., "If one day I will be forgotten, what is the point of all of my work?") This issue of the meaning and purpose of human existence is a major focus of the philoso-*

phical tradition of existentialism.

That was it! Finally, there was a name for what I was experiencing. So, now what? What the hell was I supposed to do about it? How do I fix it?

Chapter 3

Empathy

"Solace is having the same company for years while being seen as a stranger. Here, only a fool would think he had the luxury of friends."

~ Justin K. McFarlane Beau

Living life with a big heart is a double-edged sword. My heart has always been tender, with raging rivers of emotions that often felt larger than myself. Marching full force into everything I've ever done, while getting my heart bumped and bruised, I established a career from my tenderness. Throughout time, I came to understand my intuitive, empathic wiring. I learned there is a price to pay in being a deep feeler.

A tender, compassionate heart can be an amazing gift to have, as it allows one to deeply and intuitively understand and connect with people. It is like having a highly tuned radar to the needs, feelings, and moods of others. However, when not honored, nurtured, and properly cared for, this type of heart can be ferociously susceptible to the aches and pains of the world.

The emotions of the heart described above is that of an *empath*. Dr. Judith Orloff, a dynamic leader in the work of empaths, describes them as 'emotional sponges' absorbing the world's emotions and energies, sometimes without proper filters. Kim Engel is a therapist who stated, "Empaths have a higher sensitivity to outside stimuli such as sounds, big personalities, and hectic environments. They bring a lot of heart and care to the world and feel things very deeply."

An empath can sense the energy of people, a room, and a situation, without anyone saying a word. They're also conscious of people's moods and struggles. When empaths' abilities are not managed properly, they risk wearing those moods and struggles as their own.

If you are intuitively wired, with high levels of emotion and insight, you may feel the overwhelm and sting of the empath wiring. Perhaps you don't realize what a tremendous gift you have because it hasn't been properly understood, protected, or nurtured. Empathic wiring truly needs its own secret service team to protect and guide it because of its precious, delicate nature.

Typically, empaths are not understood and accepted as *gifted*. If you're wired this way, you were probably not taught to understand or value its preciousness. Empaths may feel as though something is wrong with them, like they are too sensitive and need to toughen up. Most unsupported empaths would change their wiring if they could because it feels heavy and raw; almost as though they have a disability.

I was always *that kid*... the one who rooted for the underdog, brought home stray pets, cried over the Hallmark commercials, and stayed up late listening to my friend's problems. If sensitivity were a superpower, I'd have a cape neatly draped over my shoulders and a few extras hanging in the closet.

During the early years of my life, I must have received an invisible memo about what it means to be a nice person and a friend. I don't remember who delivered the memo, but, unsuspectingly, I abided by it. The sanctioned notice must have included critical detailed requirements such as:

- always be kind and thoughtful to others
- make sure everyone and everything is okay, at all times
- you must always be enough, but make sure you're never too much
- what other people think of you really matters
- do what it takes to make sure people like you
- accommodate the wants, feelings, and needs of others
- sacrifice what you need for the needs of others
- work really hard
- try really hard

Somewhere, somehow, those critical detailed requirements were unwaveringly determined to be the '*right things*' to do for people. They were the keys to being liked, loved, and accepted. Other people's endorsements of me became the fuel that drove me—the highly sought-after *golden ticket* to my worth. Other people's happiness and well-being became my responsibility, and my value lay solely in the shallow wells of their approval.

The emotions churning inside of me had me at my wits' end; and in a desperate leap of salvation, I drove myself into the *figuring out mode.* Though an empath, I'm also tenacious, strong, and pretty damn determined. I can be fierce and am no stranger to hard work.

Being at my wits' end had me hating what was happening. It was time to get busy managing and fixing my pain. I fought against and resisted the ache I was feeling. I would not go down without a fight. So, with wild, flailing swings, I fought like a mad dog to find comfort and solace. It was time to force solutions, inform people about *my* existential crisis, and tell *them* how *they* should help *me* and make *me* feel better!

Soapbox properly placed and imaginary megaphone perched firmly to my lips, I adamantly declared, "Everyone, listen up! It is time to hear me, and hear me good. I'm hurting and I need your help. Do your part! Claim your responsibility for my turmoil! Make me feel better! I have spent years scratching your back. So now, it's your turn. You scratch mine!"

What a sight to see, no doubt a serious force to be reckoned with.

Sound familiar? Can you relate? Have you ever wanted to shout from the rooftops, "Look at me! See me! Hear me! Help me!"?

After all I had done, it was finally time to collect and let others carry the baton for a while. It was heavy, and I was tired of carrying it by myself. I wanted them to take a turn and I needed to know they were in this race with me.

Answers and solutions were being sought from others and from the outside world. I unloaded my turmoil and made them responsible for my meltdown and my recovery from it. Not only had I laid down the friendship baton, but I also began to clobber them with it, too. I had unknowingly taken their well-being on and now I wanted them to take on mine.

I was weary and fatigued. My loud, demanding pleas turned into anger, defeat, and sullen expectations. I had surrendered my personal power; perhaps, never even knowing I had such a thing. I wanted love and support to show up externally and in the ways I expected them to. Others were being held responsible for my needs and feelings, but none of them were having it.

Having no idea I had the power to make tough calls and the necessary changes, I was lost in a storm. My eyes were firmly focused outside, blind to recognizing that I was the one who desperately needed to change. It never occurred to me that my ways of relating were the ones that needed to be assessed and redirected. Every single morning, the mirror reflected the real problem; and I had absolutely no idea.

Not only had I received invisible memos, but I also had written a few somewhere along the way, as I declared the unspoken friendship guidelines. If you're in my tribe, there are going to be some new rules: show up, be nice, be thoughtful, and be considerate. I'll be that way, but you need to be that way too. I applied a friendship mold to each of my relationships and expected others to fit into it. I read the memo; therefore, I assumed everyone else must have read it, too.

People became confused by my mood, annoyed with my altered behavior, and dismayed by my attitude. They didn't understand, any more than I did, what was happening. They didn't seem to like that I wasn't managing things or working hard on our relationship. Mostly, people were puzzled. Changing the dynamics and asking for some return on my investments, didn't seem to be something they appreciated. I'm sure my chaotic, meltdown approach didn't help very much.

My resistance was strong, the blame was thick, and the resentment was seething. My world, as I knew it, had crashed.

Have you reached a point of desperation? Do you feel depleted? If your world is crashing, it may be time for you to take a good, hard look in the mirror. View the ways you've been relating to others and assess your expectations.

First look at where you are right now and answer the questions below to begin the process.

I am over-functioning and over-managing in relationships.	
True	*False*
My relationships are defined by:	
Quality	*Quantity*
3 ways I define quality relationships are:	
1.	
2.	
3.	

I am an empath.	
True	*False*
3 ways being an empath serves me in life are:	
1.	
2.	
3.	

3 ways being an empath has been difficult for me in life are:
1.
2.
3.

I need to protect and nurture my empath qualities.	
True	*False*

3 ways I can begin protecting and nurturing my empath qualities are:
1.
2.
3.

Chapter 4

Connecting

"A connection is the energy that exists between two people when they feel seen, heard, and valued; when they can give and receive without judgment and when they derive sustenance and strength from the relationship."

~ Unknown

Since you've made it this far, we must be speaking the same language. You feel my pain, and trust me, I feel yours, too. Have you reached the brink? Do you want to step aside to allow everything to crash down around you, letting the pieces fall where they may? Are you sick and tired of managing it all? Are you waking up to the fact that people, places, and things never can, and never will, fulfill your emptiness? If so, this ache inside of you deserves your full attention.

Sound the sirens, call in the troops, bang the gavel, do whatever you must to declare notice. It is time to call your life into order. It is time to suit up, show up, and claim responsibility for yourself. It is time to pay attention to what you're doing and why you're doing it.

Your old script was written from the absurd invisible relationship memo. You have an opportunity to create new marching orders; specific terms of engagement that will no longer prioritize the best interest of others. Your name is now at the top of your list.

As empowered by this as you may be feeling right now, I believe it is my duty to tell what comes next. I don't say this to scare you, but to prepare you for some very real pain you are about to experience before you are able to free yourself from your old ways. James A. Garfield said, "The truth will set you free, but first it will make you miserable." What misery was I about to face before the healthier version of me was finally free to emerge?

In all my torment, I waved my imaginary white flag and willfully surrendered the clutching and clinging to my old ways that had been sustaining any illusion of life and relationships. I let go of people, effort, forcing solutions, and figuring out what I, and others, should be doing. The woman with all the answers, the open arms, and revolving emotional door was finally bare, there was nothing left to give.

As though the heavens had opened and the angels sang, I took the world of hurt I was in and placed it at the foot of the imaginary holy altar. Perhaps for the very first time in my life, I began to look up and within, instead of outside of myself. External circumstances had failed me, and it was time to look inside of myself.

This figurative long look in the mirror revealed an empty, depleted woman who had no idea who she was, nor what her needs were.

It was time to take a good, hard look at who I was, my motives, feelings, and needs. Life was calling me to stop doing what I used to do, and instead, focus solely on spending time alone to explore what I wanted and needed. The word *selfish* reverberated through me but was quickly rebuked with the realization that this is about salvation, preservation, and survival.

Without the hustle and bustle of activities and people, I sat alone with my inner demons... the demons that had unknowingly been driving the ship and navigating my life for a long, long time. The demons nipped at my heels and echoed slithery messages of being unlovable and unvalued. I had pleased and performed all throughout my life, thinking it would ensure my place in the world. I was terribly mistaken.

Quiet solitude was painful. It felt like a permeating sense of rejection and unworthiness that I couldn't soothe, comfort, nor deny. Those demons seemed to be sitting around the campfire singing their jolly tunes of defeat and loathing; singing cheers to one another because they had finally brought this strong woman down.

In the past, my role as the Social Manager created distractions that kept those voices at bay and gave me a sense of purpose and belonging. Martyred management of others and sacrificial focus on their needs was driven from misinformation, childhood training, my own emotional pain, and lack of self-love. How could I not have seen this?

I never knew I had a personal responsibility to manage my own needs. I had poured into people to fill their cups, yet mine was dry and empty. It never occurred to me to check my own tank, to see what I needed in order to refuel. I never knew I could be more selective, assess for reciprocation, and value of my efforts.

I had invested heavily into relational accounts and sacrificially living because I was taught it was the polite way to behave. I was depending on those relational accounts for my rainy day of need, only to be slapped with the harsh reality that there would be no return on my relational investments. The accounts were empty, and I was emotionally bankrupt. All these years, all my efforts, all my attempts to build relationships gave me a tragically overdrawn account; and I had been the one who allowed it!

Hearing an impactful inspiration that pisses me off is usually evidence that I really need to listen to it. So, when I heard the question, “What if the purpose is in the pain?” I scoffed at that bullshit thought because I wasn’t ready to look at its deeper meaning.

What purpose could all of this serve? How could I possibly be growing and healing from my guts hanging out and my life being turned upside down? And yet, I knew...

The healthier version of me is a sincere believer that most everything happens for a reason. I believe life is a school that we are privileged to attend and learn valuable lessons. You have a choice whether, or not, to listen and learn. However, I assure you, if you choose not to listen and learn, life will heat up until it becomes too painful to ignore. Life wants to be heard, and it wants you to pay attention. Ironically, many people tend to learn the most through agony and torment, not through pleasure.

So, what if your exact circumstances are meant to teach you incredible lessons? What if your greatest pain is the precise curriculum required to bring you to a new level of learning, loving, and relating? What if your gut-wrenching feelings are trying to help you? What if you are the cause of your greatest pain by resisting what life is showing you?

As I asked myself those same questions it sounded like crazy talk. Yet still, something deep inside of me knew it was true, even though I didn't like it.

Can you relate? If you find yourself in the same boat, I believe you are being called into an intense season of redefining. You have a choice. Are you ready to do life differently?

What if you started to listen to what your feelings are telling you? What if you stopped criticizing and judging yourself? What if you grew curious and inquisitive about your thoughts and emotions? What if you take time to sit with your thoughts and emotions to honor and befriend their messages? What if you let go of the fuss and the fight? What if you begin trusting the divine nature of life? What if you start creating your happiness? What if you become your top priority?

The invisible memo you received may be as thick, complicated, and dysfunctional as mine was; or, maybe not. Either way, let's shine some light on your old script. Let's look at your thoughts, patterns, and habits that aren't serving you anymore. This way you can let go and redefine.

The following are terms of my old invisible memo:	
Be agreeable	
Accommodate others	
Make sure people have what they need	
Be nice	
Listen to other people's opinions	
What other people think of me matters greatly	
Work hard at relationships	
Be enough for everyone, but not too much	
Put others' needs before my own	
Include everyone	
Deny my feelings to take care of others	

3 feelings the above terms and conditions evoke in me are:
1.
2.
3.

3 insights my emotions are telling me are:
1.
2.
3.

5 terms and conditions I need to let go of are:
1.
2.
3.
4.
5.

3 behaviors I need to let go of are:
1.
2.
3.

3 positions (roles) I need to let go of are:
1.
2.
3.

3 people, places, or things I need to let go of are:
1.
2.
3.

3 thoughts I need to let go of are: *(Consider your inner demons.)*
1.
2.
3.

I want my new script to read: *(Create your new terms and conditions.)*
1.
2.
3.
4.
5.

6.
7.
8.
9.
10.

Take a deep breath. How do you feel after completing the exercises above?

Now that you have some clarity, start putting your new script into action. Practice it and use words, body language, and eye contact to help you feel more comfortable. Changing habits and rewriting your thought patterns can feel weird, ruffle some feathers, and take time to settle into. The sooner you begin, and the more you honor your own feelings and needs, the sooner it will become more comfortable and natural. Your old script has expired, and your new script is waiting for you to write it.

www.AllysonBlythe.com

Chapter 5

Kindness

"The greatest gift you can give somebody is your own personal development. I used to say, 'If you will take care of me, I will take care of you.' Now I say, 'I will take care of me for you, if you will take care of you for me."

~ Jim Rohn

Digging into core values and searching my motives, thoughts, and attitudes, I became curious about this thing called *kindness*. I started looking for role models. Mr. Rogers, now he was kind; however, I was no Mr. Rogers. But hey, who is? There's Jesus, Mother Theresa, and Gandhi; of course, they are in a league of their own. The digging continued.

Since a working definition helped define my crisis, maybe a working definition would help me find healing. Aristotle defined kindness as, "helpfulness towards someone in need, not in return for anything, nor for the advantage of the helper himself, but for that of the person helped."

Seriously? Kindness has no advantage to the helper?

That seemed more like altruism than kindness. Oh hell... How was this even possible? How, with over four decades on this earth, had I gotten the basic concept of kindness so wrong? My understanding of the core value of kindness finally became crystal clear.

It was evident I had serious issues with being good and nice. These *nice girl* issues had been my way of behaving my way into others' approval, acceptance, and future goodwill. This deceptive protocol must have been part of the ridiculous invisible memo from long ago.

My existential crisis stemmed from not knowing, honoring, and protecting my true value. Perfecting, performing, pleasing, and proving fueled my illusion of confidence, belonging, and mattering. My kindness came with an equally disturbing agenda, hidden with secret expectations and ulterior motives. All-in-all, I wanted approval and to be liked. This wasn't conscious or malicious by any means. I simply thought, *if I am kind and helpful, others will naturally reciprocate*. Simply put, if I prove you matter to me, I will matter to you. I had been using the guise of kindness with an overall motive of, *if I scratch your back, someday you'll scratch mine*. Evidently, that is not kindness. The invisible memo was wrong again.

Your ways of functioning in the world may be kind; however, look honestly at your kindness. Does it come with hidden expectations or an agenda? Is it an attempt to matter, to be included, or to be liked and well-regarded? Is your kindness a way to not feel (tragically) alone? Are you giving to others what you actually need yourself? Are you hoping others will show up for you in the same ways you show up for them?

Beyond anything else, know this: You are the one who is most capable of meeting your needs. Others cannot know you when you do not truly know yourself. Nobody can fill the void that is deep within you. No one can nurture your aches of unmet needs and unresolved pain. As you take a deep dive into your behaviors, patterns, and motives, you may begin to see a layer of truth that you're using your behavior as a means of seeking love, attention, and belonging.

Being an approval junkie will drive your thoughts, emotions, decisions, functionality, and relationships. Approval sucking often stems from not rigorously loving yourself. The absence of self-love and self-worth leaves you hungry for acknowledgment and validation from the world at large. Approval and acceptance from others become your measuring stick for personal value. Therefore, self-betrayal begins as you learn to ignore, disconnect, and dishonor your truest self.

Relationships are unique with individualized parts. Like an old family recipe, what ingredients are you using in your relationships? Are you someone well-stocked with thoughtfulness, consideration, kindness, generosity, and sacrifice? These are rich ingredients, and when measured properly, can create amazing relationships. The overuse of any ingredient can spoil an entire recipe.

Not everyone performs the same in relationships and in life. We don't all follow the same rules. Every ingredient does not need to be granted to every person. You get to choose what you want to offer different people at different times.

People tend to show up the way they desire others to show up for them. For example, you probably give love the way you want to receive love; and when you don't receive it your way, you are left confused and distraught. You may have written a personal formula for relationships. Consequently, you won't recognize how others are showing up for you in their own way. People will always show you who they are and what you can expect from them in the way they interact with you.

Adoration, attention, approval, and acceptance are all healthy, typical human needs. Who doesn't enjoy being liked? The question becomes: *How far are you willing to go in order to gain approval*?

It was a warm summer day and I was about ten years old. In the boring, lazy days of nothing to do, my friends and I decided to set up a lemonade stand. Something simple that reflects childhood innocence became a defining moment in my life. You see, the tender heart of mine could overthink and overcomplicate even the most basic situations. I felt backward and uncertain in group settings, trying hard to fit in, but not sure what to do or how to act.

They elected me with the responsibility of flagging down the cars. There wasn't a worse role than that for an uncertain, tenderhearted kid who simply wanted to match her peer's coolness. As uncomfortable as I was, I knew this might be my chance to really prove myself; to finally fit in and show everyone I was worthy of being in the cool crowd. So, I agreed to be the flagger, despite my inner voice screaming, *Don't do it!*

It was a busy street, yet my best efforts had failed to stop a single car. Todd, an older neighborhood boy, began the commentary, blaming me for the lack of the traffic's cooperation. The others laughed at Todd's commentary. However, I did not laugh; instead, I tried harder.

As a small red Nissan rounded the corner, I was hopeful that this was the car that would stop. This car would be the one that wins the glory of the first cup of lemonade sold and my ticket into the group's awe and appreciation. I was wrong, and quickly my heart sank as the car sped past.

In all of Todd's ten-year-old coolness, he hurled insults at the car and flipped the driver the bird. The other kids laughed wildly in their rebellion. I was uncomfortable because I didn't like that sort of behavior, but Todd seemed confident and the other kids seemingly agreed.

The next car drove by without hitting its breaks; so, taking the coolness cues from Todd, I flew my middle finger up towards the sky as the driver sped by. I was stunned when Todd smacked the back of my head and shouted "What are you doing? You can't act like that and expect people to stop and buy lemonade! What is wrong with you? You, dumbass!" The voices of the others echoed Todd's reprimand.

I was sickened, not only by my own behavior, but also by the fact I did the same thing the cool kid did, and it won me humiliation. Todd's punitive talk was no comparison to my own: *What is wrong with me? Why did I do that? What did I do wrong? Why can Todd do that, but I can't? Why do they hate me? Why did he hit me? I am such an idiot. Why isn't anyone sticking up for me? Why didn't that damn car stop?*

I had gone against my own instinct to act out of character; and now, everyone knew how uncool I was. I don't know if I was more devasted by Todd and the others, or myself.

Moments such as these are defining. The worst form of self-betrayal is acting against yourself to seek the approval of others. You must always respect and honor what is in your best interest. When you don't, your far-reaching efforts to gain acceptance lead to patterns of proving and pleasing. Eventually, your efforts will drive you into the ground or to looney land. Acting against yourself, fleeting approval, being liked, and fitting in are temporary and short-lived. As Brené Brown clearly defines, "There's a big difference between fitting in and belonging... a big, big difference."

Here's an important news flash: You are allowed to have needs. Needs drive everything you do; yes, everything. Equally important, you deserve to be in relationships that support, feed, and nurture your best interest and highest well-being. It is essential to understand your own needs, to take responsibility for them, and tune into your expectations of others. Holding people responsible to meet your needs is unfair and unrealistic, especially if they are unspoken.

Despite how you may have been taught and trained, you alone are responsible for knowing, communicating, and meeting your own needs. It is up to you to assess what you're doing, why you're doing it, and how well your actions serve you. If you are connected to people who are chronically unwilling or unable to meet your needs, it may be time for some serious reassessing. If you're waiting for other people to step up, to change, or to hear and help you, the wait will be long and weary.

It was humbling to realize that long after the tender age of ten, I was still acting in ways to fit in and gain approval from others. I was acting in ways that I believed *I should behave*, so others would like me more and my sense of purpose would be ensured. Though I can be incredibly kind, my neediness and skewed motives sometimes took charge, driving my endless hustle to secure first place in the popularity contest.

This was embarrassing, humbling, and filled me with regret. I had been taking too much responsibility for others and not enough for myself. Like Humpty Dumpty, my pieces had fallen, and I was waiting for others to put me back together again. I had been functioning from a place of unworthiness and neediness. Even more, I wasn't managing my boundaries; nor did I know I needed to have them. Equipped with this humbling perspective and empowered understanding, I had a starting point to begin a new path; a new way of relating.

As an adult, and still cocooned in my nest of solitude and introspection, I began tuning in. For the first time, I surrendered my desire to fit in, to appear *oh-so-nice*, and efforts to constantly do everything right. Now, I was paying attention to my own gauge and measuring my own feelings and value. Instead of always trying to include everyone in everything, I became mindful of who and what I really enjoyed. I started being deliberate about when to say "*yes*" and when to firmly say "*no.*" I concerned myself less with what other people thought, and I began weighing only my opinions.

How much time are you spending on things that really don't matter? What kind of hoops are you jumping through to fit in? What are you doing in efforts to be liked? How far have you twisted and tortured yourself to gain other's approval? Are you ready to let go of the chronic drive to connect and be included?

I assure you, there is another way to get what you desire and need. I encourage you to preserve your time and energy spent on performing and pleasing. When you begin to discover what truly makes you happy, while being mindful of your motives, your life will begin to change. Genuine happiness isn't something you read about in fairytales. It becomes an actual opportunity and natural consequence of properly managing your life. Your daunting habits, lingering pressures, and looming obligations begin to lift. The plaster you use to paint on your smile will chip away. As you begin functioning from a place of genuineness, you will notice the corners of your mouth will naturally turn upward. Even more, your words will be deliberate and gentle, your spirit will be light, and your laughter will produce easy and deep authentic sounds.

Redefining your terms and conditions for behaviors, boundaries, and relationships will offer you strength, clarity, and satisfaction. However, you may need to lighten your social schedule, spend more time alone, and shrink your contact list. If you can withstand the discomfort and sit in the stillness of the in-between, you will be alright. You will get to the other side to establish your new norm; a new way of relating to others. Although, first, you must enter the gates of self-discovery, endure the echoing voices of your past, and sit through the discomfort of the unfamiliar. As you do, you will feel more connected, fulfilled, serene, and rooted. The less you do and the more intentional you become, the fuller your cup will be; and ironically enough, the more you will be able to pour into others.

Finally, you will be living intentionally to give others what you truly have available to give, rather than what others expect from you. You will function without depleting yourself from those sacrificial attempts to please and fit in. You will notice, the more you take care of and focus on yourself, the more kind you will become. It may seem backward, but the martyred sacrifice of taking care of others is not going to lead you to peace and happiness. Gaining a clearer understanding of who you are, what you want, and your deepest core values will fill your cup and allow you to get back in the game! This is your journey of healing and restoration while redefining your acts of love and kindness.

3 ingredients I use to relate in relationships are:
1.
2.
3.

My definition of kindness is:

5 ways I can begin showing kindness to myself are:
1.
2.
3.
4.
5.

5 motives I have for being kind are: *(Dig deep and be honest.)*
1.
2.
3.
4.
5.

When I assess my motives, I can detect the ways I've misused kindness.		
Rarely	*Sometimes*	*Often*

Being kind causes me to feel unappreciated and undervalued.		
Rarely	*Sometimes*	*Often*

5 things I expect to get in return for my kindness are: *(If you say "nothing," I encourage you to dig deeper. Most people have hidden expectations, even if it's a simple "Thank you" or a subconscious hope of future reciprocation.)*
1.
2.
3.
4.
5.

5 areas in my life where I can begin saying "no" are:
1.
2.
3.
4.
5.

As you begin saying "no," use the space below to record your process.			
The Situation	**My Response**	**How I Felt**	**The Result**
A friend asks me to help move	*I said no*	*Stress, guilty, relieved*	*I am proud of myself for valuing my time*

It is my hope that these exercises enlighten and empower you into a new way of showing up; of relating and connecting through your true essence; to end the hustle and contortion of congeniality and popularity; to offer your full, unyielding self to the world.

Give credence and expression to your journey by using this book, and perhaps, another journal that is dedicated to your personal process so you can honor and celebrate your growth. Pour out your heart and soul onto the pages. Color, write, scribble, doodle, draw, it doesn't matter. No one is watching, and besides, this is your path!

Chapter 6

Fed-Upness

"Don't ever underestimate the actions of a person who is fed up. Last chances don't come with warnings."
~ Unknown

Life is the greatest teacher and the learning is never-ending. At times, the lessons in front of you are easy ones, simply packaged, all tidy and neat. Some of the guidance can be rigorous and challenging, forcing you to new levels of consciousness and skill. Then there are the lessons that can only be learned from the face down, head buried, fetal position of agony and defeat.

Regardless, life honestly works in your favor and is offering endless opportunities to teach you the lessons you need to learn. As an adult with free will, you get to decide if you want to learn the lesson, listen to the redirection, and to accept the correction. No matter how good, how successful, how much money, or how smart anyone is, we all have lessons to discover and paths to travel. No one comes through life unscathed, and everyone wears their battle wounds differently.

My existential crisis was absolutely no exception.

Having risen from the ashes, and now, standing firmly on the other side, I can see how necessary the entire process was. Looking back at that painful life curriculum, I'm filled with wonderment and appreciation. I laugh at the resistance I had to the entire experience because it was excruciating, and I took it personally. This life lesson was packaged like a shit sandwich that I couldn't digest; and yet, it helped birth my most necessary insight, changes, and life's work.

I cringe at the way I held others hostage for my happiness and how I believed my healing rested in their hands. The whole process was messy, and my fuss and resistance made it even more wicked. Only now can I fully embrace the fact that, just like a butterfly trying to strengthen her stunning little wings, I needed every single step of my painful journey. I needed it to breathe life into a healthier, transformed life, to give a voice to new ways of relating, and to birth this powerful book.

I've heard it said, "The teacher teaches that which she most needs to learn." Oh, the irony of my epic meltdown. Consciously choosing to sort through pieces of my existential crisis granted me a new lens through which I began understanding life. My compassion for people shifted as I began to see the signs and symptoms of crisis in others. It became apparent that I was not the only one who had received outlandish notices about relationships; and certainly not the only one who was experiencing confusion about the terms and conditions of relationships. It was as if the whole world was equally baffled.

I was sitting with my client, Laura, and through her tears, she seemed to plead, "I don't understand. I'm a really good person. Why the hell do I keep meeting these people who seem to take advantage of me?"

Greg was another story. He was long past the tears, and he was in a full-blown rage. "What the fuck is wrong with people? Why is it that every time I try to help someone, I end up getting shit on?"

Then there was the humorous approach that Mary tried to take. "Where is it? Where is the label? Do you see it? Obviously, everyone else in the world can see the word 'sucker' written somewhere on me!"

The seething resentment, depletion, and exhaustion gave me evidence of other peoples' over-functioning, tangled expectations, and misguided kindness.

Scott's situation was serious. He had been diagnosed with Bipolar Disorder by his medical doctor. She had urged him to see a professional so he could start a medication regimen right away. Thankfully, my office was his first stop. He ranted about his life-long patterns of following the rules, the pressures he felt to be a good person, the community boards he sat on, daily efforts to check on his elderly parents, and the hours worked to maintain a prestigious income for his wife who was a *lover of things.*

Scott was exhausted. Recognizing that he was nearing a dangerous edge in his life, he started to consider taking a demotion at work. Even more, he began to explore his lifelong interest of bike riding, rather than the boring committee at church. On more than one occasion, he firmly told his wife "no" when she asked more from him. Aghast by these sudden behavioral changes, his family was certain he had lost his mind. According to them and the doctor, his behavior was strong evidence of a manic episode.

Two sessions in, I handed Scott a folded piece of paper. On it was my official diagnosis. I wanted him to be prepared for what he was about to read because I had seen it before, and I knew the seriousness of a disorder like his if untreated. He took the paper carefully, somewhat defensively, and slowly unfolded it, obviously trying to brace himself for what he was about to read. His smile was one of relief as he read the diagnosis aloud:

"Fed-Upness"

Scott, and too many others like him, were fed up with overdoing it in relationships and in life. People can only pour in a certain amount before they run dry. 'Fed-Upness' is not a mental illness, nor is it selfishness; it's common sense.

Are you fed-up? Can you see your own signs and symptoms of this dreadful disorder? The warning signs may not register on Web MD, but I'm sure you may be able to self-diagnose.

5 of signs and symptoms I feel from Fed-Upness are:
1.
2.
3.
4.
5.

Like a 100-watt bulb that suddenly illuminates the darkest room, my clients began to see what the real issues were. We talked about their understanding of, and intent with, kindness, connection, and relationships. We investigated their motives, feelings, and expectations. They were challenged to look within, to take responsibility only for themselves, and explore their core values and needs. They began to see their patterns of performing, pleasing, and over-functioning in attempts to secure their place in the world. We looked at what they were giving, who they were giving to, and the reasons they were giving. Ultimately, they had a frame of reference, defining words, and a lens through which they could comprehend their feelings and destructive patterns.

It was like a news flash. They weren't horrible, selfish

people who weren't sacrificial enough, or who didn't know how to love. They weren't crazy, bad, dysfunctional people; they simply had been following terms and conditions that were counterproductive and depleting. Simply put, they are kind, thoughtful, sweet souls who had the rules all backwards and who were worn out. *Finally*, my clients had an understanding and compassion for what they were experiencing.

Imagine having a plethora of food and generously giving it all away. Would you shame yourself when you finally became hungry? Certainly not. Family, religious, and social systems don't typically offer the same credence to emotional needs that they do physical needs. The rigid, sacrificial standards that define being a *good person* doesn't allow for balance and self-care. Instead, those standards contribute to emotional depletion.

Awareness is, perhaps, the most powerful tool in your toolbox. It leads to profound conversations in my office and promotes massive changes in the lives of my clients. For the first time, people understand how misguided they were in their attempts to help, connect with, and love others. They were creating changes in their lives and starting to recognize how they had mismanaged themselves and their relationships.

Clients continue to walk into my office with signs and symptoms of Fed-Upness. They are in a crisis, riddled with thoughts, stories, and the burden of selfishness, heavily medicated, and misdiagnosed. They believe they are bad people. They are plagued by the haunting messages of what it means to be *nice* and *good*.

Continuing my mission to educate, equip, and empower those I work with, I knew the trek needed to continue and the scope needed to broaden to reach many more Scotts, Marys, Lauras, and Gregs in the world.

One of the first conditions for you to consider is that your well-being and satisfaction are your number one priority and responsibility. As you embrace this truth, you'll surrender your victimizing story and step out of the blame game. Hard calls must be made. Deep feelings will be felt. Tough conversations will need to be had... Perhaps this is what being an adult is all about.

Chapter 7

Adulting

"Adulting is the path you have to walk and stray.
You meet a lot of people, but no one is there to stay.
You have to fall. You have to get up.
Make things happen and make them setup.
You have to catch those dreams you saw in your sleep.
You have to walk down those roads, no matter how steep. You have to learn to be alone during hard times.
You need to lose yourself sometime.
Witnessing all this, night and day.
This is what adulting is all about,
to walk alone and stray."

~ Ritesh Bisht

"Adulting is soup and I am a fork."

~ Unknown

Imagine spending 18 years in training for your future. Day in and day out, training for a position, only to arrive on the first day with the dreadful realization that you are horribly under qualified. Welcome to adulthood! If someone were to clarify the job description for adulthood, I think it would be written something like this:

Wanted

Full-Time Adult

The qualified candidate must have the following:

- *strong communication skills*
- *independent thinking*
- *effective decision-making*
- *strong coping strategies*
- *negotiation skills*
- *problem solving resources*
- *resiliency*
- *time management*
- *ability to listen and understand people*
- *function autonomously as part of a larger whole*
- *build quality connections*
- *weed out riffraff*
- *manage difficult situations, especially with difficult people*
- *attention to detail*
- *honest and trustworthy*
- *assess feelings and needs of self and others*
- *act in one's best interest*
- *maintain spirit of compassion and empathy for self and others*
- *accurately assess situations as they are (rather than how you think they should be) and act accordingly*
- *maintain a calm spirit while avoiding pressure and frantic hustle*

Damn, it's hard being a grown-up! Where are the lesson plans and standardized tests that measure your growth and progress along the way?

We're not taught this stuff! There are no established programs to educate kids about social, emotional, and relational skills that really matter. Where are the resources to effectively train everyone for the largest responsibility of life... being an adult? The day-to-day tasks of knowing how to manage life seems like a lot at times. Adding the pressures and expectations of relationships can be maddening, especially under the old terms and conditions of those invisible relationship memos.

So, where to begin? With everything we are uncovering, what now? How do you rewrite years worth of history, learning, and patterns ingrained so deeply that you may not even realize you have them?

To me, being an adult means:

Effective adulting skills I possess are:
1.
2.
3.
4.
5.
6.
7.
8.
9.
10.

3 adulting skills I lack are:
1.
2.
3.

This is your opportunity to decide for yourself the skills and resources you need to effectively manage your social, emotional, and relational well-being. *Finally*, a chance to write your own job description as you take ownership of your mind and heart, while acknowledging complete responsibility for your life. The ingredients required in this process include honesty, authenticity, genuineness, vulnerability, courage, openness, willingness, acceptance, and trust. The rest will unfold on its own.

Learning to pay close attention to what you're feeling and the thoughts you entertain is a great starting point. Trust yourself and trust that life is directing you as you bring all of yourself on this journey. You deserve your full attention. Show up fully, not perfectly.

During this work, your relationships will be examined, your motives will be confronted, and your patterns will be transformed. You will come to a season in life where you must look at what you're doing, and why. You will dive deep into taking an honest look at your feelings, thoughts, and behaviors. You will walk through your healing into the corridor of a new life. Once you crossover, you will be able to joyfully stand alone and fully embrace your value.

Chapter 8

Attention

"You are not clingy, or needy, or silly for having needs for affection, affirmation, and attention. Those needs aren't an embarrassing outgrowth of your low self-esteem or depression; or whatever messy emotional issues you may have going on. That's just basic shit that people need from each other. We, of course, should not make our partners responsible for meeting all our emotional needs—it's not someone else's job to make you happy. But, inside a healthy relationship, being able to show affection, pay attention, and demonstrate 'you are amazing and important to me' is a pleasure; not some task or burden."

~ Unknown

"I continue to believe that if children are given the necessary tools to succeed, they will succeed beyond their wildest dreams."

~ *David Vitter*

My goodness, look at the ways we've judged, ridiculed, and scrutinized the need for attention, recognition, acknowledgment, and appreciation in our world: *needy, attention seeking, drama queen, haughty, hot-*

shot, big mouth, smarty pants, full of themselves, bitch pseudo, egotistical, bullshitter, showoff, narcissist, big timer, braggart, blowhard, flaunting, grandstanding, know-it-all, attention whore, big ham, bag of wind...

The first moment breath enters your little lungs, all your fundamental human needs come alive inside of you. Children thrive when given attention and nurtured. In the ideal world, these basic needs are securely and consistently met throughout life. But, let's be real, ideal doesn't really exist.

Life's natural course will pinch, pull, steamroll, defeat, and compromise children. In the eyes of a child, a parent's disapproval can seem psychologically torturous because it threatens their sense of safety and stability in the world. Kids learn ways to acclimate and do what they can to ensure their needs for attention and connection are met, one way or another.

Roles played, behavior used, performance learned, appearance perfected, and accomplishments achieved are the ways of the world for children. They learn about themselves and establish their sense of worth within the family trenches, and then advance into larger arenas. Most kids look for messages that reassure they are accepted and loved. They will even avoid situations that threaten a parent's approval. These well-rehearsed behaviors become solidified in the way children relate in the world.

The process of individualization is essential for children. We've all heard of the terrible twos and understand it is a time of development. Even more, it is a time when children assert their voice and work to establish tiny levels of independence. Children need to test their wings to learn about themselves and the world, and their place in it.

Adolescence is another time when a child's world begins to expand. They look beyond their parents and home life to understand who they are and how they perceive the world at large. Sometime between the ages of eighteen and twenty, these young adults stretch their wings (once again) as they step out and soar into the world.

Emotional development stages are equally essential to the physical milestones of learning to walk and talk. Achieving autonomy is pivotal in shaping a child's permission, safety, and competency to explore who they are and how they interact. Additionally, social, academic, and religious cultures influence a child's worldview and supports or hinders their personal permission to explore themselves and the world.

Parents are the most significant contributors in a child's world and, by far, have one of the toughest jobs on earth. It is a parent's responsibility to shape the mind, body, and spirit of these little creatures, all while managing their own lives, careers, relationships, health, and the whole shebang.

To further complicate it, parenting is typically an 18-year, one-way street. Parents pour into their children far more than children should ever pour into their parents. It is an understatement to say parenting is a 'thankless' job. Despite it all, parents take on the challenge of raising these little people into happy, healthy, well-adapted, big people. Most do it happily and with honor; perhaps, not ever fully knowing the task they are called to do.

Effective parents want to teach their children to be nice, helpful, and accommodating. Of course, it is important for kids to learn manners and how to be considerate; however, there is a fine line in shaping the spirit and personality of a child. Knowing how to instill manners, respect, and compliance, while empowering a child to use his or her voice, can be a delicate line to walk, even for the best of parents.

Life happens. Sometimes children are overridden, ignored at times, and misunderstood. Parents don't have time to patiently wipe every spill, kiss every bumped knee, and calmly assist with each assignment. They are stressed and busy, and kids require a lot of time, patience, and effort.

Kids watch and assess the behaviors, tasks, and roles they need to assume to sustain parental lifelines of approval and attention. Perhaps they were cute, polite, and helpful; or maybe being strong, athletic, or smart won the parental accolades.

What ways did you learn to gain attention and approval? Were you allowed to have a voice in your family? Were you allowed to have opposing opinions? Was there conflict or tension when you went against the family norm? Did you find yourself dismissed, mocked, discouraged, or even punished in your attempts to differentiate and test your wings?

As an adult, I have a need for attention.		
Rarely	*Sometimes*	*Often*
I have been shamed for being an attention seeker.		
True	*False*	
I'm embarrassed to need attention.		
Rarely	*Sometimes*	*Often*

5 actions that gained me attention when I was a kid were:
1.
2.
3.
4.
5.

I was safely and consistently paid attention to as a kid.		
Rarely	*Sometimes*	*Often*

It was safe for me to separate from my family and have my own opinions.		
Rarely	*Sometimes*	*Often*

Here's the deal, just because we get older our human needs for approval and acceptance do not dissolve. Those needs are alive inside of us when we turn 1, 21, 41, and even 71. However, attention-seeking doesn't have quite the same permission for a 32-year-old as it does for a 2-year-old. Somehow, these core needs get misconstrued and ridiculed, as though you should've grown out of them by a certain age and time. As I reflect on my childhood experiences, I can clearly see the age I had *outgrown* my need for approval and acceptance.

My parents were hosting a dinner party when I was about eight years old. I remember innocently feeling the festivities of the night. The evening was growing long, and the visitors were lingering. As the guests gathered to collect their coats, it seemed the perfect opportunity to perform for them. So, I began to twirl and dance across the living room.

One gentleman who was a stranger to me, spoke loudly, perhaps saturated with evening spirits, "You, young lady, are being a *show-off*; and I must say, no one likes a show-off." The wind was taken from my sails, and my spirits were dashed as I was introduced to my first dose of humiliation and shame.

The sting of devastation and confusion was evident, although I didn't even realize what a show-off was and why it was a terrible trait. However, I was determined never again to be labeled a show-off. So, the deal was sealed; I would never draw that kind of attention to myself and would never risk those dangerous emotional waters of shame and humiliation ever again.

It doesn't take much to impact the heart, mind, and spirit of a child. One small message can have profound effects that become solidified within their little minds.

I remember sitting with my client, Jasmine, who was in her late twenties. Listening to her feelings and struggles, I quickly spotted her yearning for attention. As I reflected the need back to her, she responded as though I had slapped her across the face. Still mortified by the sting, she quietly questioned, "Shouldn't I have grown out of that by now?" Oh, my goodness, what have we done in our society when we create shame around such a basic human need?

The typical, run of the mill course of growing up is impactful enough. Yet, when a child is exposed to abusive, neglectful, or stressful circumstances (intended or unintended), the scars are palpable as they learn their place through a damaged lens. Poverty, parental illness, death, divorce, absence, addiction, physical, emotional, sexual, or any level of ongoing tension impacts the belief system, and developmental and coping strategies. Children learn ways to function and adapt to these circumstances with such limited perspectives, resources, and coping mechanisms. How easy it must be for them to draw faulty conclusions such as: *This is my fault. The world is not safe. Adults aren't reliable. I must manage this on my own. How can I fix this?*

Children's hearts and minds are exposed to the world's muck, long before they can understand and effectively deal with it. Those beliefs become imprinted into their psyche and identified as truth. Sadly, kids don't magically unlearn those messages upon reaching adulthood. Their distorted perceptions become deeply rooted into the foundation of their every existence.

I was a junior in college in Dr. Evans' Sociology class. One day, we participated in a social experiment, where we were each given a headband with a label on it. We were instructed not to look at the label and to spend twenty minutes relating to others in the class, based solely on the label that was written on the headpiece. *Cool, this is easy*, I thought, feeling excited about something different.

With my headband securely in place, I wandered around the room reading labels such as businessman, a person with AIDS, stay at home mother, young African American male, homeless woman, homeless man, a pervert, and many more. People chatted, made faces and gestures, shook hands, and found different ways to engage with one another. It was fascinating to watch, and I found some of my own belief systems surfacing... beliefs I hadn't been aware of until I began interacting.

The activity continued, but I was feeling troubled and growing disturbed. No matter how hard I tried, people weren't engaging with me. Each time I approached someone, they seemed to look right through me. I kept at it, assuming my label must be something terrible, but surely someone would be willing to give me a shot. The process continued, and each time I was ignored it hurt a little more. These people were my classmates and friends, yet not one person was seeing or relating to me. I knew it was an experiment, but it felt horrible.

As we continued, I was less and less willing to try. I found myself longing for some form of connection but avoiding people at the same time because the sting of rejection cut deep. Before long, I moved myself to the outskirts of the room. As I watched everyone else gain at least some level of connection, I eventually sat down on the floor, feeling defeated and horribly alone amongst a room full of people. The minutes seemed to turn to hours as I waited for the entire thing to be over. It may have been the longest twenty minutes of my life. Finally, Dr. Evans called the class to order. With headbands still on, she asked us to identify what we thought our label was, based on how others had interacted with us.

I had no idea what my headband read, but I knew that whatever it was, I was going to make damn sure I was never *that* in real life. Unable to guess at what the label possibly could be, she finally permitted me to remove the ridiculous headdress to reveal the devastating label. I could not rip that thing off my head fast enough, and seized it, as if to choke the life out of it. *Any guess what it was?*

It was *invisible*. My label was *invisible*.

Tears streamed down my face, and I realized the horror of that feeling. Perhaps that was one defining moment for me in never wanting anyone I cared about to ever feel that way. The memory haunted me for days and I could feel that hopeless, paralyzed despair; yet, it was merely a twenty-minute exercise. More than twenty years later, I can still feel the grip of it; its powers engraved. Can you imagine a lifetime of feeling invisible?

Think of something that needs to be paid attention to, nurtured, and properly cared for (plant, home, bank account, pet, lawn, vehicle, or relationship). When not properly tended to, they fade, deteriorate, and eventually die.

Imagine a tree that isn't chopped down, isn't properly watered, is exposed only to limited sunlight, and is planted in very shallow soil. The tree may try to grow in all kinds of directions in efforts to reach for the light. However, it will not be deeply rooted, healthy, and capable of bearing strong branches or nourishing fruit. The same is true for the mind, body, and spirit of a child.

Kids are not only affected by direct trauma or neglect. There is an equally detrimental experience that puts them at risk. For some children, invisible and ignored are precisely how they feel. They are raised in an environment where no one is paying attention, tuning in, investing, or pouring into them to teach them about who they are and how to navigate the world. Perhaps they go unnoticed, unseen, or unsupported; they are invisible, irrelevant, and ignored within their family.

Have you ever felt invisible? The emotions attached to feeling invisible can be subtle, and comparable to an emotional toxic mold exposure. You can't see it or smell it, but over the years, it produces real damage that can go unrecognized, unacknowledged, or misconstrued. You know something is wrong. Something is dreadfully off about the way you feel, but you can't determine what it is. Therefore, you tragically conclude, it must be you.

Sam's attempts to be seen started when he was a small boy. His desire to belong drove most of what he did. His efforts were endless and costing him, in every capacity, way too much. He reported a lifelong sense of disconnect and being undervalued.

We happened upon an interesting dynamic when discussing his family home. He reported that from an incredibly young age he slept on a small cot off the back porch. The number of kids simply outweighed the number of beds, so he found solace in that tiny spot. As we investigated further, he reported a major upheaval when, at age 11, his sister's boyfriend came to live with them. Sam's parents granted this young man his small porch haven, leaving him to sleep on the floor in a sleeping bag for the next seven years.

A lack of space easily equated to a lack of mattering, a lack of stability, and a lack of belonging. There was no hitting, and no documentable bumps or bruises. However, there was a tender heart that drew the conclusion that he didn't matter. He believed his place was easily disrupted by random people who seemed to matter more than him.

The harm this causes is often misunderstood because it is based on what *did not* happen, rather than on a specific incident, concrete facts, or physical evidence. This is very damaging to children because it is an invisible type of abuse or neglect that injures their spirit and soul. It is truly a sense of lack that permeates a child's worth.

Some kids are born into families in which they simply do not fit—square peg, round hole type of not fitting. Their wiring is different from the family norm, leaving them with a chronic sense that something is wrong with them. In their minds, *different* means *wrong.* That message becomes woven into the fabric of the child's identity.

Loneliness is one of the biggest determining factors in your well-being, health, and overall longevity. It is safe to say, connecting, mattering, and belonging can literally be a life or death issue.

So, let's dive in. Perhaps, for you, childhood sucked with evident abuse or trauma, maybe it was a sense of being invisible, ignored, or not mattering. It is time to acknowledge your past in order to grieve and understand the impact it had on shaping your feelings, beliefs, and coping mechanisms. Next comes the point when you must let go, surrender, and ask, "Now what?"

In my childhood, I experienced:
Trauma
Abuse
Neglect
Invisible
Ignored
Not Mattering

The impact this had on me is:
The beliefs I have grown to believe about myself are:
A defining moment in my life that shaped how I see myself is:
I would describe myself as:

Chapter 9

Nature vs. Nurture

"The ultimate experiment in nature versus nurture is the one who is engaged in a constant battle between what he was and what he wanted to be."

~ Larissa Lonen

"The phrase 'nature and nurture' is a convenient jingle of words, for it separates under two distinct heads the innumerable elements of which personality is composed. Nature is all that man brings with himself into the world; nurture is every influence that affects him after his birth."

~ Francis Galton

Can you hear it? Listen carefully as Lady Gaga belts out, "Baby, I was born this way!" Are you just born certain ways, or did situations happen that molded who you are? It's really a classic question. I believe it is both nature and nurture that shapes us into our magnificent, individualized souls.

You were born unique. Your wiring, spirit, personality, preferences, and talents are ingrained in your personal imprint on this world. Also, you were born into a family, neighborhood, and culture that contributed to shaping and defining who you are, the way you relate in the world, the things you believe, and the ways you cope. You are an individualized creature influenced by the world around you. So, how you were born and what you were born into sets the foundation for how you function.

Nature defines your personal preferences, tolerances, strengths, struggles, talents, etc. Just like being born blue-eyed or brown-eyed, and left-handed or right-handed, you were born with emotional and physical preferences and capabilities.

Nurture includes the environmental influences that you were born into. Kids tend to become that which they are exposed to; or perhaps, the exact opposite. Your family and cultural dynamics, along with peer and academic experiences, all influence the development of your personality, coping skills, and belief systems. What you were taught to believe, what you received attention and approval for, and how you were labeled, rewarded, reinforced, and punished, all influence your self-esteem.

Most parents aren't knowingly setting their children up for a lifetime of dysfunction and struggle. Countless messages are well-intended attempts to shape a child's compliance and character, while reinforcing cooperation and rewarding good behavior. Teaching kids to be well-behaved are not parental travesties, and yet, inadvertently, can impair a child's spirit.

Let's get real. Most parents are doing the best they can with the information and resources they have. Your parents probably weren't nurtured any more than you were. There is no training manual; no *Healthy Relationships-R-Us* store; and *Boundaries 101* is not a standard prerequisite for entering into life.

For some senseless reason, it was determined, somewhere down the line, that our educational system was best suited for things like Algebra, Economics, Statistics, English, and Chemistry. Life skills like emotional intelligence, self-awareness, personal boundaries, and conflict management aren't included in the curriculum. Nevertheless, they are the tools and skills that lay the foundation for a productive, healthy life. Perhaps it was just assumed these topics would be learned somewhere along the path of life? It's a risky and faulty assumption for sure.

Remember, attention and approval are at the core of a child's existence. Children learn their roles and use certain behaviors to understand their purpose and worth through the attention and approval they receive. As these roles and behaviors are reinforced and rewarded, they become hardwired into the very foundation of a child.

Your childhood roles may reflect your natural strengths and abilities. Other times, it is a total misrepresentation of you that causes dysfunction and misunderstanding. It is like going through the world using your nondominant hand because everyone thinks that is the way you should be doing it.

What are some of the ways you learned to function in childhood? What roles won you favor in the eyes of a parent? Below are some roles you may recognize.

The roles I played in my family were:		
Funny	*Smart*	*Pretty*
Helper	*Dramatic*	*The Good One*
Rebel	*Clown*	*The Bad one*
Cute	*Clown*	*Sickly*
Athletic	*Stupid*	*Invisible*
Use the spaces below to write in your own.		

The roles I played are an accurate reflection of me.		
Not at All	*Somewhat*	*Completely*
The roles I played highlight my natural strengths.		
Not at All	*Somewhat*	*Completely*
The roles I played were truer for my family than for me.		
Not at All	*Somewhat*	*Completely*

The roles you played are important to consider, along with their authenticity for who you are. Again, none of them are inadvertently wrong or bad. They do, however, create an impression on how others understand and relate to you, along with the standards and expectations they have for you. The roles you play create a lens through which you see the world and how the world sees you.

Being conscious of the roles you play, how well they suit you, and the message they portray are important to understand. You get to write the script of adulthood; therefore, these roles can be reassessed and rewritten.

Male vs. Female

"Men are not more immune from emotions than women; we think women are more emotional because the culture lets them give free vent to certain feelings; 'feminine' ones, that is. No anger please, but it's okay to turn on the waterworks."
~ Una Stannard

Childhood messages and early training are interwoven into the very fabric of social and familial patterns. They are subtle and indirect; beginning with the toys children are encouraged to play with, the sports teams they are allowed to join, the nicknames they have, and the colors of their clothes and bedrooms. Family and cultural systems reinforce what are acceptable and unacceptable behaviors. Messages become ingrained, to the point, you may not even realize how your habitual ways of relating and functioning affect your relationships and how you behave in the world.

Females tend to get recognized and rewarded for their kind, considerate, and compliant behaviors. Our culture is one where women have much more permission to feel and take care of themselves than men do. We have book clubs, journals, Oprah, mani-pedis, spa days, girls' trips, and a therapist on speed dial. Though times are steadily changing, historically, women have been rewarded for being incapable and weak, while being reinforced for their sacrifices and martyrdom.

In theory, we encourage the strength, determination, and assertiveness of a woman. We proclaim her rights as an independent sexualized human. Yet, in real life, when that same woman shows up, she is quickly judged as a bossy bitch who is just a whore. There is still judgment, ridicule, and stigma attached to an assertive, successful, and sexualized woman. Just sit back and watch her walk into a room. What are your first thoughts?

Men are up against another set of standards and rigid fine lines. They do not have the same permission or freedom to experience emotions or self-care, without appearing weak. Men are reinforced for their strong, capable qualities and their ability to suck it up, tough it out, and be a man. Their worth is connected to their strength, accomplishments, and earning potential. Men are trained to deny and suppress their emotions; but are expected to be wildly romantic and available for the *knight in shining armor* role.

Men are trained with role models like Steven Seagal, the Marlboro Man, Arnold Schwarzenegger, Clint Eastwood, and Superman. Women want their men emotionally available, but not with too many feelings or needs of their own, because then they would be a wuss and needy. Men are expected to be strong, confident, and capable of managing their own feelings and needs, while being attentive, understanding, patient, grounded, and available for their partners. Watch a man cry or expose any vulnerability and you will see the judgments fly!

What was your experience with learning the feminine and masculine roles of your family and culture? What family roles or conditioned behaviors won you the most favor? What messages did you get about independence, emotional expression, or asserting personal preferences? How well do these messages fit with your true self?

My childhood role models were:
1.
2.
3.

I was raised to believe men should have the following 5 characteristics:
1.
2.
3.
4.
5.

I was raised to believe women should have the following 5 characteristics:
1.
2.
3.
4.
5.

Now as an adult, I believe men should have the following 5 characteristics:
1.
2.
3.
4.
5.

Now as an adult, I believe women should have the following 5 characteristics:
1.
2.
3.
4.
5.

Chapter 10

Conflict

"Peace is not the absence of conflict,
but the ability to cope with it."
~ Mahatma Gandhi

"If you avoid conflict to keep peace,
you start a war inside yourself."
~ Cheryl Richardson

How fast do your feet hit the floor when you hear the words: "We need to talk."? Do you automatically assume you've done something wrong? When you hear the word *conflict*, what's the first thought that comes to your mind? What picture takes shape in your mind when someone is upset with you? Is there an overwhelming feeling of dread or fear when you have a disagreement? Do you automatically assume someone else's mood has something to do with you? Do you personalize situations or the moods and reactions of others?

You can almost hear the sizzle of peoples' skin as they volley the hot potato back and forth, trying not to be the one stuck dealing with it. Avoidance, ignoring, denial, blame, and minimizing may be ways you learned to deal with hard issues in your life. Parents deeply influence their children with the ways they manage tension, work pressure, financial strain, and conflict. What happens in a marriage, between family members, and within the parents themselves, shapes a child's understanding of stress and conflict management.

Watching a parent fly into a rage is terrifying to a child. Seeing an adult fall to a heap on the floor is overwhelming and can instill helplessness. Being subjected to neighborhood complaints or family gossip can be way too much information for little ears. A parent who uses a child as their confidant or pseudo partner can lead to emotional incest. Sweeping issues under the rug leads to a tumultuous foundation; and avoidance causes issues to seep out in other areas of life. Kids are watching, drawing constant conclusions, shaping their beliefs, and learning impactful lessons.

While some families demonstrate obvious dysfunction in the ways they handle tension and conflict, others aren't quite so obvious. When someone tells me that they had a perfect childhood, I call bullshit. Don't get me wrong, some kids are born into really cool families who help shape them into becoming equally cool adults. However, no family or childhood is perfect. Families who raise their children without ever demonstrating how to manage tension in healthy ways aren't doing their kiddos any favors because their children will grow up to be big people who have no idea how to cope with disagreements. Typically, words such as perfect, ideal, magical, etc., indicate family issues that have been ignored, minimized, denied, or dismissed.

Parents don't automatically know how to handle feelings, tension, and conflict any better than you do. What they observed and concluded is what they know how to pass down. They can't teach something they don't know. When conflict is managed in unhealthy or ineffective ways, it has negative consequences. Therefore, people develop negative associations such as *all conflict is bad* or *if we argue, they will leave*.

This is how conflict was handled in my family:	
This is how my family members managed themselves and their feelings when there was any kind of stress or disruption:	
Mom	
Dad	
Siblings	

The conclusions drawn from my above answers are:

These are my feelings about conflict:

Looking back with adult eyes, incidents like the ones you wrote above may not seem like a big deal. Perhaps you dismissed them as, *just the way it was.* However, I encourage you to look at the messages you received and how they influenced the way you handle tension and conflict.

Are you fearful and avoidant when it comes to disputes, or do you charge into them like a raging bull? Some people avoid conflict at all costs and will do anything to smooth it out. Others will roll up their sleeves and start swinging madly.

Perhaps you rock from one side of the pendulum to the other. Do you stuff things down until you can't take it anymore and then emotionally or physically blow? Have you found yourself tearing into some poor, pitiful bystander who just happens to cross your path? Let's look at your approach.

When there is an issue that needs my attention, I:	
Distract	*Avoid*
Ignore	*Attack*

When there is an issue that needs my attention, I feel:	
Fear	*Dread*
Overwhelm	*Panic*
Rage	*Hostility*
Worry	*Relief*

This is how I handle conflict:

These are some topics or situations I want to begin handling differently:
1.
2.
3.
4.
5.

Chapter 11

Emotions

"We try so hard to hide everything we're really feeling from those who probably need to know our true feelings the most. People try to bottle up their emotions as if it's somehow wrong to have natural reactions to life."

~ Unknown

"Emotions make us human. Denying them makes us beasts."

~ Victoria Klein

It's a wonder why people continue to procreate. Children are hard to raise, and I can imagine every single parent asks the inevitable question, "How can I make sure I don't screw them up?"

Seriously, parenting is the greatest responsibility one could possibly undertake; and we've already covered the impossible line parents must walk. Some people are naturals and are really darn good at it, others, not so much.

Part of raising a well-rounded child is teaching them to

pay attention to their physical cues. Helping kids understand their bodies and sensations of pain, fatigue, and hunger is essential. Effective parents teach children to listen to their bodies when it comes to their biological needs. Potty training, daily naps, and three square meals are all ways parents teach, train, and develop little people.

Most parents do not approach hunger, sleep, or even potty accidents, as evidence the child is misbehaving because they understand the physical requirements of kids. These are all normal physical needs that take time, understanding, and training.

Though most parents could earn a gold star when addressing the physical needs of their children, it may be another story when it comes to their emotional needs. Emotions are a complicated web where parents often get tangled. Emotional management is another level of parenting that is probably more essential than physical management. Yet, parents are confused by, overwhelmed with, and reactive toward the emotional and sensory needs of their little people. Unfortunately, parents (and general society) don't honor the same understanding, permission, and respect for emotional development as they do the physical. Kids are sometimes expected to function with adult understanding, skills, and maturity, long before they have the capacity to do so.

Parents want their kids to cooperate, so they negate,

minimize, ignore, or bulldoze over a child's emotions to get them to behave. It may be a rare occasion, but it is bound to happen. For example, kids scream that they're hungry, and parents tell them to shut up and go to bed. Kids don't pick up their shoes, and parents tell them they're ungrateful little bastards. Kids get hurt when they don't listen, and parents tell them it serves them right. It happens to the best of us, but nonetheless, it has a profound impact on kids; and children get jacked up somewhere along the line.

How many times when a child complains they're hungry, does a parent offer the retort, "I just fed you two hours ago"? A child shivers, "I'm cold," which earns them the response of, "How can you possibly be cold? It's 75 degrees in here." Perhaps, in the best efforts of reassurance, parents tell their children not to feel a certain way or that the feeling is wrong. Ironically enough, it is moments like those when kids actually do listen to their parents.

Naturally, kids need to listen to authority, behave obediently, and follow rules and agendas. Most of their early life is based on external direction and compliance to what others decide for them. However, kids don't always fall right into line or shift gears easily from one thing to the next.

A child's ability to emotionally regulate is as complicated as the algorithms they'll be expected to learn later in life. They seem to come with their own needs, feelings, understandings, paces, and timelines. Kids can be labeled as rude, disruptive, naughty, and disrespectful when they have big emotions they don't know how to regulate. Parents may not know what to do with this perceived misbehavior, so they add to their child's distress by yelling, ignoring, punishing, or chastising their kids to enforce compliance. Even on the best of days, parents may find themselves resorting to punishment, shame, yelling, and even name-calling just to get a child to cooperate. This is all in the natural order of parenting.

Inevitably, the intuitive powers we're born with tend to get crushed throughout the course of childhood. Kids learn to listen to voices outside of themselves and squash their inner voice to comply and keep out of trouble. Kids aren't typically educated, nor empowered, to use their innate wisdom (gut senses) to navigate life, nor are they encouraged to decide for themselves in most situations. Punishment, yelling, and shame are used to reprimand children, rather than understanding, soothing, regulating, assuring, teaching, or role modeling for them. Years of this disconnect can wreak havoc on the soul.

Well, heck, now what? Are you simply doomed because your spirit got squashed as a kid? Is it really all your parent's fault, after all? *Of course not.*

The first step of the healing process is *awareness*. Your body is intuitively wired, and it is never too late to tune into gut senses. Your senses may be very well hidden, and you may not know what you're looking for. However, you can learn to befriend your intuition by paying attention to what it is telling you; and more importantly, follow its guidance.

"When you bury emotions like that, you're only pissing them off— making them stronger, because you're burying them alive. They don't like that, and one day they'll make sure you don't like it either."
~ Rob Thurman

Your body is the 'teller of truth' and will offer signs and symptoms of distress and disorder. The intuitive, emotional body is the exact same. It will offer signs and symptoms as cues for you to know something is wrong and needs your attention. So, pay attention to what your body is telling you.

Signs and Symptoms of Distress & Disorder

- Irritation
- Guilt
- Stress
- Strain
- Worry
- Exhaustion
- Depletion
- Overwhelm
- Resentment

Ignoring, overriding, minimizing, excusing, justifying, or even worse, blaming yourself for any signs and symptoms is a deep self-betrayal. Just how ignoring physical signs and symptoms can lead to a more severe diagnosis, so is the case with emotional warnings. Early intervention is the key to your overall well-being. When you imagine your emotional warnings to function like a scale that is at its tipping point, it is easier to resolve problems easily, quickly, and more effectively.

My signs and symptoms of emotional stress are:	

When feelings arise that I don't know how to deal with, I tend to:	
Ignore	*Distract*
Avoid	*Numb*
Ridicule	*Express*
Investigate	*Justify*

Emotions I feel most comfortable with are:	

Emotions I feel least comfortable with are:	

Hopefully, the moment you touch a hot stove, you recognize the danger and quickly remove your hand. The same action must happen when life's problems arise; feel the discomfort, recognize the problem, and take immediate action to resolve it.

Can you imagine forcing your hand to remain on a hot stove, as you tell yourself that you're making too much of it and a better, stronger person would be able handle the pain? Nonsense, for sure! Don't do that to yourself, emotionally!

A hot emotional stove is a warning sign that needs your attention and intervention. Learning to listen, embrace, and investigate the warnings is an essential life skill. Emotions are powerful, intuitive cues that deserve your full attention.

Your body, mind, and spirit are intuitively wired to

offer information and guidance. You have an internal sense, a knowing. When listened to, referenced, respected, and trusted, your intuition is your best advocate and wisest guide.

The problem is, people seldom listen to their intuitive gift, much less nurture, consult, or give it authority. When you shame your emotional cues as though there's something wrong with you (signs of weakness or a character flaw), you devalue your source of personal power.

Learning to trust yourself and use your emotions as your guide is a vital step in this process. Investigating your feelings allows you to stay open and curious and offers you profound insight and clarity. Your feelings are trying to tell you something. Maybe your thoughts and behaviors are out of whack; maybe there is something going on with someone you care about; maybe there's something off about a situation. Honoring your feelings empowers you into deeper levels of knowing and self-trust.

On the next page is a list of various emotions with a short description of the possible message each emotion is trying to deliver to you. Take a few moments to read over each. *Have you been recognizing the messages the emotions have been telling you?*

Following the messages is a quick exercise to further help you identify your regular emotions and messages.

Feeling	Possible Messages
Anger	Perceived injustice, someone or something has gone wrong. Anger is legitimate and can also be a mask for deeper, more vulnerable emotions
Fear	Safety, danger, risk, worry, and anticipation
Sadness	Grief, loss, heavy burden
Happiness	Joy, love, calm, satisfaction with the way things are going, and needs are met
Hurt	You've been wounded; a boundary has been crossed
Disappointment	Loss of plans or expectation, things worked out differently than you had hoped
Resentment	Expectations, waiting too long, depletion
Guilt	Maybe you're off your personal mark; or perhaps you're buying into other people's pressures or expectations
Worry	Anticipating, fear of what may or may not happen, trying to predict or control the future
Discomfort	Something is off that needs your attention

Emotions I feel regularly are:	These emotions are trying to tell me:

I can begin honoring my emotions by:
1.
2.
3.
4.
5.
6.
7.
8.
9.
10.

Chapter 12

Commodities

"Opinions are the cheapest commodities on earth. Everyone has a flock of opinions ready to be wished upon anyone who will accept them. If you are influenced by opinions when you reach decisions, you will not succeed in any undertaking."
~ Napoleon Hill

When you hear words such as *important, valuable, treasured, cherished,* and *precious,* what images come to your mind? When I mention words such as those, and refer to life's commodities, most people's immediate thought is money.

We live in a society that is driven by the almighty dollar. From an early age, we receive the following messages about money: *save it, spend it, earn it, squander it, borrow it, steal it, hoard it, invest it, fear it*. Family messages about poverty, wealth, competence, intelligence, and worth, stem back generations. We are tightly bound to role models, core values, and long-standing beliefs within the family and cultural systems associated with *the buck* we have *in the bank*. Money is a powerful definer, and the training starts early.

The tooth fairy rewards children with a hidden treasure under their pillow. Piggy banks are cute and a great way to store change. Games such as *Life* and *Monopoly* introduce savvy adult concepts and allows players to test their hand at wheelin' and dealin' skills.

Financial gurus like Dave Ramsey and Suzie Orman have based their careers on helping people learn and earn, while wielding financial tips. There are apps, programs, economic classes, and a whole slew of tools to help inform and educate people about the use and management of money. There's even an entire legal system put into place for people who misspend or find themselves in a financial crisis.

Money holds serious emotion and energy-filled messages about security and value. We assign character assets to the wealthy and make assumptions about their lifestyle. There are messages about the deserving and undeserving; and even *The American Dream* is connected to opportunities to earn.

It is a fact that people can have mega-full bank account and still be unfulfilled, anxious, and miserable. Money, though rightfully associated with happiness, does not directly create it. So, if happiness isn't about money in the bank, what is? What do you attribute to happiness?

On the following page is a place for you to define happiness according to the way you see and feel it.

I define happiness as:

In the process of rebuilding my life, I began questioning all I *thought* I surely knew. I let go of the assumptions, habits, beliefs, and trained thoughts, and became curious. I started looking closely at the values I was holding and the behaviors I was tolerating.

I went back to consult Siri's all-knowing powers. I asked her about joy, personal value, happiness, and life purpose. Amid the quest, I accidentally stumbled across the word *commodity*.

"Siri, define commodity." Here's what she stated, "*a useful or valuable thing*." The wheels started to turn, and the questions began to whirl in my mind. I knew I was onto something. I began asking myself the following questions; and now, I encourage you to answer them.

Who comes to mind when thinking about someone who is happy?		

With my life having been filled with many kind and helpful acts, why do I feel depleted and unhappy?
1.
2.
3.
4.
5.

If money isn't the source of happiness, what is it that happy people do and don't do to remain happy?	
Do	***Don't Do***

What do happy people have or don't have?	
Have	***Don't Have***

What do their lives look like?

With my life having been filled with many kind and helpful acts, why do I feel depleted and unhappy?
1.
2.
3.
4.
5.

Wielding my handy dandy toolbox, I pulled out the most effective of all tools: *Awareness*. I began to investigate and pay attention to this thing called *happiness*; and people who seemed to have it, and those who didn't.

Though, typically, I am not a dedicated researcher, I am a pretty clever cookie. So, here's what I gathered: Happy people seem to be fueled by three primary commodities that have nothing to do with money. With much focus on the almighty dollar, these three valuable assets tend to go unrecognized. They are rarely recognized, taught, acknowledged, prioritized, respected, nor celebrated. However, when spent wisely, can add incredible significance to your life.

The three commodities are:

- Time
- Energy
- Effort

"When we contemplate buying something,
we usually ask the price of it, then decide whether
or not it is worth that much to us. But when we expend
time and energy, we often just go ahead and pay."
~ Ruth Stout

Imagine having more than enough time. Imagine using each minute and hour to honor and fulfill you. Imagine reserving your energy for the sake of your well-being. Imagine focusing on people, places, and things that sustain you. Imagine allowing relationships to effortlessly flow. Imagine...

How are you expending your time, energy, and effort? How could your life change by evaluating the ways you spend your time, energy, and effort? What could happen if you start to evaluate your return on investment? How would your life be more satisfying by pinpointing which commodities are sucking you dry?

I know... I know... I can hear it now. "Isn't it *selfish* to think you should assess an ROI in relationships? Wouldn't a good [loving, honorable, religious] person offer their time, energy, and effort without worrying about what is in it for them?"

Well, maybe. You're free to see it however you choose. What I know for sure is, many people are working way too hard in relationships for the sake of others. Even more, many people never look at the toll it's taking on them. You may be *over-functioning* with too many people, in too many ways, for way too long. Self-care has tragically been mistaken as selfish. Allowing yourself to show up on your own list of priorities has been labeled as entitled. Let me lay down the bullshit card one more time.

Hopefully, every time you swipe your credit or debit card, you have some idea of what's in your bank account. Access to your bank account is carefully guarded, balances and passwords are tucked away for safekeeping, and only the most trusted souls can gain information about your account. Has it ever registered that you can be just as protective with your time, energy, and effort... your emotional well-being?

Do you invest in people, places, and things without checking if you really have it in you to give? Are you underestimating the value of your time, energy, and effort? Have you ever stopped to ask yourself: *How much is this going to cost me?*

Do you offer wide-sweeping affirmative responses such as “sure,” “absolutely,” “of course,” and “without question,” before investigating the price to your most valuable commodities? Rote responses such as those are habitual and accommodating, putting you into high risk of careless overspending. They send dangerous messages about the lengths you will go to support another, without considering the toll on yourself. If you are protective of your almighty dollar, be equally mindful of your other commodities.

Martyrdom may have been generationally role modeled for you. I witnessed it in multiple capacities for extended generations; and I’ll tell you, it didn’t lead to happiness for anyone in my family. It bred angry, bitter, and resentful people who continued to give.

So, the keys to happiness are time, energy, and effort. They seem to be the common denominators for living joyfully and maintaining healthy relationships and personal well-being. People who are conscious of their spending in these three areas seem to have an ability to monitor, assess, and gauge these assets. Moreover, they intuitively, trust their ability to navigate life and protect their best interest. They say “yes” when they want to and offer a “no” without lingering guilt. Also, they are able to define healthy parameters for their giving.

In the next chapter, as we dive deeper into commodities, you will learn more about expending your time, energy, and effort. Before moving on, given what you have learned in this chapter, go back to the beginning of this chapter to reassess your answers to defining happiness and its true source.

Chapter 13

Time, Energy, & Effort

"Personal development is the belief that you are worth the effort, time, and energy needed to develop yourself."
~ Denis Waitley

Time

Time is the most treasured commodity you can offer someone. It is of paramount importance; and perhaps, the single most determining factor of the quality of your life. There are 1,440 minutes in a day, 10,080 minutes in a week, and 524,160 minutes in a year. Once you spend it, you can never get it back. One could imagine that it is every person's dying wish to have more.

Time is one of the most charitable resources available, yet it's treated with pint-sized regard. Our society has become one in which we anesthetize and distract our way through time with things that add no value to life.

Ask someone how they are these days, and you're likely to hear, "Busy!" through a furrowed, martyred brow. Stillness is a stranger, and rushing has become commonplace. The distress of it all is worn as an imaginary badge of honor to display your sense of competence and worth.

Chaos, urgency, and crisis are frequently assigned to trivial situations, while neglecting and delaying that which truly matters. There is an obscure fear of falling behind, along with dread of perceived consequences for not keeping up with whomever and whatever. People regularly function in a low-grade panic, haunted by the chronic sense of lots to do and much to manage.

Watch people standing in line and see the way they grab for their phone and tap their feet at the discomfort of waiting. We have become resistant to stillness; and terrified of it, too. With immediate gratification, entitlement, forever flowing information, and hundreds (if not thousands) of options, there is a chronic urgency to be doing, getting, and achieving—all while really going nowhere. We've become a society who doesn't know how to remain in the present.

My challenge to you is to track where your time is being spent. On the following pages there is a time log for you to fill out. Many think they adamantly know where they are spending their time. This handwritten exercise is an eye-opening opportunity to really view your time in black and white. Like a financial advisor calls you out on your financial spending, I'm calling you out to be honest about your mindless timewasters.

	Mon	Tues	Wed	Thurs	Fri
6:00 am					
7:00 am					
8:00 am					
9:00 am					
10:00 am					
11:00 am					
12:00 pm					
1:00 pm					

2:00 pm					
3:00 pm					
4:00 pm					
5:00 pm					
6:00 pm					
7:00 pm					
8:00 pm					
9:00 pm					
10:00 pm					

These are the top three ways I spend my time.
1.
2.
3.

Energy

Energy is the amount of attention you devote to someone or something. It is your peace of mind... the emotional and mental space you allow a person or situation to occupy. Simply put, energy is where you place your focus.

Are you allowing others to live rent free in your mind? How much thought, consideration, attention, and worry are you willing to offer? How hard are you working on relationships? How much space are you allowing someone or something to occupy in your mind? Are you spending way too much emotional energy?

Below and on the following page, highlight the Emotionally Energetic Expenditures (E.E.E.) you are overspending.

Getting Upset	Over-Thinking
Worrying	Planning
Consideration	Thoughtfulness
Problem Solving	Offering Solutions
Explaining Yourself	Extending Loyalty
Pleasing	Chasing After

Checking Up On	Accommodating
Seeking Love	Seeking Attention
Seeking Approval	Personalizing Other's Behaviors
Entertaining Conversations	

Emotional energy can easily be confused with love. The manage, fix, and control patterns you're accustomed to might be your only examples of love. The difference between helping and enabling is a fine line that's easily blurred.

Watching someone you love struggle or suffer is excruciating. Your assistance may seem essential. You may believe your problem-solving and management skills will help rescue someone. You may think it's your responsibility to offer support. You may feel something tragic will likely happen if you just stand by. Deciding not to get involved can be like watching someone step into traffic without intervening. It's terrifying to think about what could happen if you don't interfere. You may feel guilty if you choose not to get involved, even if their downfall is a consequence of their own behavior.

There is a big difference between feeling bad about something vs. feeling guilty. Feeling *bad* (sad, worried, frustrated, anxious, furious) when something difficult happens is normal, understandable, and completely appropriate. Guilt, however, is indicative of having done something wrong. Feelings of guilt for not helping someone is a clear sign you are trying to own the responsibility of someone else's life. Learning to separate uncomfortable feelings from the guise of guilt is a vital emotional tool.

Detachment is the ability to lovingly disconnect yourself from a person or situation, while surrendering the righteous belief that you know what's best. It is not a reflection that you are uncaring and selfish. It's simply trusting that everyone has a supreme guide, and you aren't it.

Detachment can be confusing and scary, and sometimes downright awful. You may mistake detachment as neglect, irresponsible, not caring, or selfishness. The opposite is true. Choosing not to get involved, rescue, over-function, and over-manage someone else's life is one of the most loving acts you can do for yourself and the other person. Allowing someone the dignity to live their life, make their own decisions, and endure the consequences of their behavior may be what promotes their personal awakening.

Something is not always better than nothing. Do you find yourself settling, excusing, justifying, and consistently eating the shit sandwiches others serve? If so, you might be trying to avoid the discomfort of being alone. Do you often pull up a seat at the shit sandwich buffet? If so, you might not know how to act in your own best interest and are afraid to be alone. Be conscious of what you're settling for. There are no worse aches than feeling deserted in a relationship and selling yourself out.

I spend too much energy on people.		
Rarely	*Sometimes*	*Often*

I have a hard time detaching from people I care about.		
Rarely	*Sometimes*	*Often*

Other people's issues occupy a lot of my mind.		
Rarely	*Sometimes*	*Often*

I mistake bad feelings for guilt.		
Rarely	*Sometimes*	*Often*

Effort

Effort is the way you physically engage with others. It displays the lengths you will go to be considerate or helpful. It includes how you're willing to behave, perform, and interact with someone, and how hard you'll work to be of assistance.

Spending effort may include:

- Calling to check on someone
- Buying things for others
- Paying a bill for someone

- Driving someone around when they don't have a car
- Driving someone around when their car is in the shop
- Driving someone around because they got a DUI
- Allowing someone to move in with you
- Taking someone to an appointment
- Handling difficult conversations for someone
- Taking someone out to eat for their birthday
- Paying for meals every time you go out with someone
- Doing someone's laundry
- Cleaning up after someone
- Running someone else's errands
- Making phone calls for others
- Doing all the talking
- Being the only one who initiates contact with family or friends
- Maintaining secrets and excuses
- Listening to someone's problems
- Hosting or managing holiday events
- Hosting or managing social events
- Buying gifts
- Bailing someone out
- Giving money
- Initiating the conversation after a conflict
- Initiating intimacy
- Justifying yourself

- Justifying someone else's behavior to others
- Driving long distance for a date
- Driving long distance for elderly parents
- Driving long distance for abusive parents
- Driving long distance for a meeting

In all the above examples, it is not inadvertently unhealthy or wrong to say "yes" to helping. You are in charge; you get to decide what you do or don't want to do. Your responses deserve careful consideration. Be mindful of the blanketed affirmative responses we discussed in chapter twelve *(sure, absolutely, of course, without question)*. When someone seeks your help, take time to understand the efforts needed from you once you get involved. Taking this time allows you to assess how you will be affected emotionally and energetically. Also, understand, you have the right to change your mind.

Another point to consider is the overall health of the relationship with whom you're helping. What is the frequency of your help? Are they racking up serious frequent flyer points when it comes to helping them? Are you the only one they ever rely on? Would they be there for you in your time of need?

Do you give until it hurts, then believe doing more is the best solution? Does it feel impossible to allow people to struggle? Are you a fixer who neglects to cope with your own emotions? Is the fear of being alone driving you to be a people pleaser? Do you do everything possible to avoid others being angry at you, or even worse, leaving you? These types of relating are codependent, counterproductive, and exhausting.

You Might Be Overspending on These People

- Friends
- Partner
- Children
- Grandchildren
- Parents
- Siblings
- Ex-partners
- Extended family
- Job
- Boss
- Coworkers
- Church
- Church Members
- Neighbors
- Strangers

The following is where and with whom I tend to overspend.	

www.AllysonBlythe.com

Chapter 14

Points of Awareness

"Awareness is all about restoring your freedom to choose what you want, instead of what your past imposes on you."
~ Deepak Chopra

Most behaviors are well-trained and habitual. You may be running on autopilot, overspending from years of conditioning. Let's dig into this to look at why you do what you do.

Reasons You May Be Overspending

- Family roles, pressures, and expectations
- Learned behaviors
- Habit
- Social and cultural norms
- Avoiding conflict
- Avoiding difficult conversations or decisions
- Fear someone will be angry or think badly of you
- Fear of abandonment
- Religious expectations and teaching
    - Spiritual messages of martyrdom

    - Spiritual teaching of helpfulness and forgiveness
- Guilt
    - A belief that you *should* be helping or fixing
- Patterns of pleasing
    - Doing for others to feel better about yourself
    - Finding your purpose in taking care of others
- Wanting people to like and approve of you
- Blame
    - Someone telling you it is your fault or responsibility
- Confusion
    - Not understanding boundaries or when to set them
- Safety
    - Feelings or history of threat, coercion, or intimidation to yourself, property, or something you care about. (See a trained professional for help and direction about any kind of safety issues.)

Conscious awareness of your patterns will help shine light on your deeper needs that drive your behaviors. This is crucial to help effectively navigate your decisions, thoughts, and behaviors. Furthermore, being aware of your needs puts you in the driver's seat of your life. Once you are in the driver's seat, you will begin working with yourself, instead of against yourself. Moreover, you will no longer be dependent on someone else to rescue you.

3 Essential Points of Awareness

1. Know your signs and symptoms.
2. Understand where you overspend.
3. Know why you overspend.

The top five reasons I overspend are:
1.
2.
3.
4.
5.

Like a well-designed dance, these dynamic points of awareness embolden you to oversee your own life. Committing to the necessary changes means you are changing your dance with people. If you are like most, your accustomed dance has been poorly executed, well-rehearsed, and deeply ingrained, and needs to end.

As essential as awareness is, it can also be overwhelming. It's not always easy knowing when and who to help. It can feel baffling and leave you uncertain. As though there is an invisible pendulum, people tend to swing far to one side when first setting limits. They overcompensate for many years of overextending. All-in-all, they assume they can't say "yes" to anything, anymore.

Learning new ways of relating to others can feel like writing with the opposite hand... awkward, messy, and frustrating. It can sometimes make situations seem worse, piss people off, and leave you feeling bewildered. If boundaries were easy to set, we would all be setting them and living much better lives. Since they aren't easy to set, nor operate, in the next chapter, we will dive deep into setting and maintaining boundaries.

Chapter 15

Boundaries

"If I repeatedly allow my boundaries to be violated, I'm a volunteer, not a victim. It is my job to be with people who are affirming and safe and limit my interactions with those who aren't."

~ Hope for Today p. 311

There is much fuss about these things called *boundaries*! A word and concept so common, yet few people understand what they are and how and when to set them. Effective boundaries have nothing to do with telling others what they can and cannot do; that is control. Boundaries refer to your inner limits and how you will respond if those limits are crossed. It's about your behavior, not theirs.

Imagine a line that separates the good from the bad; the healthy from the unhealthy; the wanted from the unwanted. Boundaries help you clarify what you like and what you don't like; what feels okay and what doesn't. They help you define what is in your best interest mentally, physically, emotionally, relationally, financially, and spiritually. Like buoys defining and protecting you in safer waters, your personal limits are meant to keep you from venturing into precarious relational waters; waters in which you are dangerously at risk of going back to old patterns.

Boundaries encompass your words, behavior, and follow-through, which all support and reinforce your limits. Words without reinforcing behavior become empty threats; ultimately ruining your creditability.

Boundaries Defined

Professional Version:

"The ways you relate to others and allow others to relate to you that feel safe and acceptable; and how you will respond when someone passes those limits."

~ Allyson Blythe

Real Life Version:

"Mind your business and own your shit,
and let other people mind and own theirs."

~ Allyson Blythe

Siri is going to pipe in on this one too:

"Something that shows where an area ends, and another begins: a point or limit that indicates where two things become different."

~ Merriam-Webster

Boundaries are about maintaining your side of the street by knowing, understanding, and taking responsibility for your desires and needs. It is about handling difficult conversations and situations with personal honor. Even more, it is about speaking and acting in your own best interest, even when it challenges others. Boundaries have everything to do with you and very little to do with other people.

Living to accommodate others, over-functioning, and preforming destroy your chances of living your best life. Those actions will never get you on the road that leads to healthy relationships. Placing your boundaries in the hands of others and blaming them for not allowing you to have boundaries is victimhood.

Boundaries require you to let go of the victim mentality, martyred functioning, and childlike passivity. They require your adult self to show up, take things into account, assume full responsibility, make tough calls, and be in charge of your interactions with others.

Are you waiting for the real adult in your life to show up? Do you want someone more *adultier* than you to tell you what to do and when to do it? Join the club! Navigating relational waters can be tough, scary, and lead to deeper emotional seas that feel far above your head. Grab your life preserver, suit up, and show up. This is *your* job to do!

This is your opportunity to rewrite your script to clarify what truly works in your life. It's okay to be wobbly, afraid, or uncertain at times. Remember, those feelings are cues and indicators that progress is being made. If you're feeling unstable, it probably means you are getting it right, because new ways of functioning will be unfamiliar to you and shock those around you. Their shockwaves will affect you in the short-term. However, in the end, you will better know how to weather the storms.

I want to start setting boundaries with the following people:
1.
2.
3.
4.
5.

I want to put the following new boundaries in place:
1.
2.
3.
4.
5.

The follow up actions or consequences I am willing to set if these boundaries are not respected are:
1.
2.
3.
4.
5.

The following are the new ways I want to relate to others:
1.
2.
3.
4.
5.

Some areas in my life where I can begin saying "no," instead of "yes" are:
1.
2.
3.
4.
5.

As you begin saying "no" use the space below to record your process. *(I filled in an example for you to get you started.)*			
The Situation	**How I felt saying "No"**	**How I felt after saying "No"**	**The overall result of saying "No"**
Will you help me move?	Guilty	Free from stress of having to do something.	I am proud of myself for valuing my need for less activity.

As you begin new ways of relating and assessing situations prior to saying "yes" or getting involved, use the space below to record what you feel.

The Situation	How I displayed kindness	How this made me feel	My overall attitude
Will you help me move?	I can't help, but you can borrow our truck.	Helpful, but not overwhelmed.	Good, and I don't expect anything in return.

It is my hope that these exercises enlighten you to an empowered way of showing up; of relating and connecting to your true essence; to end the hustle of congeniality; to stop the contortion of popularity; and to offer your truest self to the world.

Why boundaries are vital to your overall well-being:

- Allows you to take care of yourself
- Allows you to take care of your responsibilities
- Ensures physical, emotional, sexual, financial safety, and well-being
- Increases personal joy and happiness
- Helps define your preferences… likes and dislikes… what feels good and what doesn't
- Preserves the overall health of your relationships
- Builds self-respect and self-esteem
- Increases connection and intimacy with safe people
- Allows you to make yourself a priority
- Integrity: People can trust your "yes" and your "no"
- Clarifies communication… people don't need to guess, or mind read
- Allows you to function from a place of authenticity, rather than social or familial conditioning

Setting and maintaining boundaries is, by far, one of the healthiest things you can do for yourself and for your relationships. Most people don't realize the vast categories of boundaries that exist. Each type deserves consideration to clarify what feels good to you, and what doesn't.

The many different types of boundaries that exist are not cut and dry; meaning, setting limits is not always black and white. Boundaries can be fluid, flexible, and adaptable. They may fluctuate from day-to-day, may vary from person to person, and can change over time as you get to know someone better. How you interact with a stranger will look much different than how you interact with a sibling. Also, with someone whom you had a hurtful experience with, you might have firmer boundaries. Your willingness to do something one day may be much different on the days you've worked long hours or don't feel well. Perhaps something feels okay with women, but not with men; and vice versa. Not all boundaries are in full force, at all times, nor with all people. It is for these reasons, tuning in to your instinct is critical. Your intuition is your strongest personal navigator. Boundaries are not one-size-fits-all.

With all this talk about boundaries, let's move forward to spend time in the next chapter exploring what they really are and how they shape your relationships and your daily life.

www.AllysonBlythe.com

Chapter 16

Types of Boundaries

"I didn't set this boundary to offend, nor please you. I did it to manage the priorities and goals I have set for my life."

~ Unknown

"Setting boundaries in a relationship implies your attempt to continue the relationship in a healthy way. It's not an attempt to hurt the other person."

~ Shilpa

This chapter requires a warning label. You are about to be introduced to twelve types of boundaries. They are: physical, emotional, sexual, verbal, financial, material, time, energy, social, spatial, food, and spiritual. Due to there being so many, I encourage you to take your time getting through this chapter. You may find this is not a chapter you conquer in one sitting. In fact, you will be more successful setting and maintaining your boundaries when you practice implementing one or two congruently.

Each of the categories outlined in this chapter will help you define your preferences and how you relate to others. The first step in setting boundaries is to notice when you begin to feel uncomfortable, annoyed, or uncertain. Remember, negative feelings are important cues that deserve your attention. Even more, they are a collection of information that is likely pointing you in the direction of a boundary. Let's get started!

Physical Boundaries

Your body has natural responses that prompts you into your physical preferences. There is an instinctual reaction you have when something feels uncomfortable or unsafe. It often resonates as a feeling of uncertainty or angst, like a *yikes* or *uh-oh* feeling.

Physical boundaries encompass your comfort level with your body, touch, and proximity to loved ones vs. a stranger. For example, handshakes vs. hugs, personal space, close talkers, locked doors, open doors, closed doors, privacy, tickling, someone standing behind you, kissing in public, etc.

Physically, I feel most comfortable with the following boundaries in my home:
1.
2.
3.
4.
5.

The following physical actions trigger *yikes* or *uh-oh* responses:
1.
2.
3.
4.
5.

Emotional Boundaries

Emotional boundaries encompass your emotions and the emotions of others. They also involve knowing who is responsible for what. Emotional boundaries regard things such as: comfort level with blame, conflict, managing guilt, personal sharing, teasing, sarcasm, volume of conversation, being vulnerable, receiving feedback from others, dealing with a hurtful remark, offering advice, receiving advice, handling criticism, loud talkers, being an internal vs. external processor, specific emotional tolerance (being around someone who is really angry vs. someone who is happy or sad), etc.

I'm comfortable being vulnerable around others.		
Rarely	*Sometimes*	*Often*
I can manage well in the face of anger or conflict.		
Rarely	*Sometimes*	*Often*

I'm able to determine what my feelings are.		
Rarely	*Sometimes*	*Often*
I can detach myself from other people's feelings.		
Rarely	*Sometimes*	*Often*
Other people's moods really affect me.		
Rarely	*Sometimes*	*Often*
It's hard for me to be around someone who is sad.		
Rarely	*Sometimes*	*Often*
Sarcasm and teasing trouble me.		
Rarely	*Sometimes*	*Often*
I prefer to process situations and feelings.		
Internally	*Externally*	

I feel emotionally safe when:
1.
2.
3.

Sexual Boundaries

Your sexual boundaries are influenced by your history. They encompass your safety surrounding sex and the partner(s) you choose. Sexual health may be an indicator of the overall health of the relationship.

This is your comfort level with nudity, privacy, touch,

behaviors you'll engage in or receive, conversations about sex, sexual petting, foreplay, kissing, words used to describe acts or body parts, etc.

Sexual behaviors I feel comfortable with are:	

Sexual behaviors I feel uncomfortable with are:	

I'm able to verbalize my sexual preferences.		
Rarely	*Sometimes*	*Often*

Verbal Boundaries

Verbal boundaries encompass your comfort level with types of speech. They include cussing, volume, length and frequency of conversations, what you share and with whom, etc.

Three things that help me feel heard are:
1.
2.
3.

Three things that make me feel uncomfortable in conversation are:
1.
2.
3.

Financial Boundaries

We've already addressed the power of your beliefs, history, and feelings about money. Let's look at what feels okay with finances, and what doesn't.

Money boundaries relate to your feelings about debt tolerance, spending, investing, retirement, loaning vs. giving money (why you're giving and to whom), amount and frequency of giving, paying for things for someone and why, borrowing from others, paying your bills on time, having a savings account and how much is in it, etc.

Money and finances cause me a lot of stress:		
Rarely	*Sometimes*	*Often*

My feeling or energy about money is:

I feel financially secure when...
1.
2.
3.
4.
5.

Material Boundaries

Your belongings tend to hold a lot of emotional energies, whether you're conscious of it or not. Some people are naturally carefree (generous) with 'stuff' while others hoard or cling to them for a sense of purpose and identity. The decisions to buy, keep, or dump stuff are typically engrained and habitual, but energetic, nonetheless.

Material boundaries involve your comfort level with lending, borrowing, or giving away your possessions, understanding the physical things you hold onto and why. Examples include: loaning your car or tools, letting someone borrow personal items (toothbrush, clothes, books, etc.), clutter tolerance, holding onto Grandmother's old dishes stored in the basement, and keeping every art project your child ever created.

Material possessions overwhelm me or create difficulties in my relationships with others.		
Rarely	*Sometimes*	*Often*

I buy or keep things for reasons other than need. *(on sale, fear, obligation, just in case, impression, nostalgia)*		
Rarely	*Sometimes*	*Often*

I derive a lot of purpose and meaning from my belongings.	
Yes	*No*

I keep things based on:	
Quality	*Quantity*

Time Boundaries

Some people are driven by the clock, defining much of what they do by the hours in the day. Other people pay little regard to time or have difficulty managing it. Time is a valuable commodity; so, it's important to know your preferences to make the most of your time.

Time boundaries encompass punctuality, being late, time on the phone, spending time with certain people or at certain places, taking immediate action, procrastinating, meeting deadlines or treating them as suggestions, whether you're an early bird or a night owl, etc.

My time preferences are:
1.
2.
3.
4.
5.

Energy Boundaries

We've addressed the importance of managing your emotional energy. You may be highly influenced by the vibe of different people, places, and situations. Your fuel tank is your responsibility. It is important to assess and gauge what fills your cup vs. what empties it.

Energetic boundaries help define your tolerance for thoughts you entertain, the feelings you get from others, where you choose to put your focus, how heavily you weigh other people's opinions, the ability to stand firm in your beliefs, keeping an open mind while remaining grounded, being around negativity, dealing with different types of people, holding space for other people's problems, the moods you practice, how other people's moods influence you, watching the news, politics, listening to certain music, how you feel in any given situation, how much exposure you allow yourself, etc.

Things that drain my energy are:
1.
2.
3.
4.
5.

Three indicators that my energy is draining are:
1.
2.
3.

People who drain my energy are:
1.
2.
3.

Places that drain my energy are:
1.
2.
3.

Ways I can protect my energy are:
1.
2.
3.

Ways I can fill my own cup are:
1.
2.
3.

Social Boundaries

Some people are far more introverted than others. Therefore, people have a variety of preferences for when, where, and how they mingle with others. Being social has much to do with your need for connection, belonging, and entertainment. People can have vastly different ways they meet these needs.

Social boundaries help you define your likes and dislikes for interacting with people, places, and things, being extroverted vs. introverted, loud places, smoky environments, being around alcohol or other controversial environments, calling, texting, chatting with someone, large groups vs. one-on-one interactions, etc.

I identify myself as:	
Introverted	*Extroverted*

Three ways I like to socialize are:
1.
2.
3.

I feel most connected to people when:
1.
2.
3.

Some environments I feel most uncomfortable in are:
1.
2.
3.

Spatial Boundaries

Though these issues have been around for a long time, spatial boundaries are more relevant with the advancement of technology and things such as texting, social media, long distance relationships, etc. People have different expectations and guidelines relating to their contact with others. Some take it very personally when someone doesn't respond, while others require more solitude and separateness in a relationship.

Spatial boundaries encompass how you perceive and handle togetherness vs. separation, expectations with calls and texts, frequency and methods of contact, quality vs. quantity of time, privacy, sharing your passwords, etc.

It's important for me to have consistent contact with people who matter to me.		
Not Really	*Somewhat*	*Very Much*

I need separateness and distance in relationships.		
Not Really	*Somewhat*	*Very Much*

My preference is that people respond to a call or text within...			
5 minutes or less	*30 minutes or less*	*Within a few hours*	*Within 24 hours*

In relationships, I feel most connected when:
1.
2.
3.

Food Boundaries

Food boundaries are interesting and affect some more than others. Many people don't even know they have food issues until they start to investigate this category. Food can be very relational and emotional. It also carries different meanings depending on the family and culture. A sense of lack (food instability or inconsistency) can be significant in defining people's responses to food.

This category is about your comfort level with sharing and preparing food, who you will cook for, allowing others to cook for you, foods you will and won't eat, eating or drinking after someone, how full your cupboards must be, eating leftovers, etc.

Food holds emotional energy to me.	
Yes	*No*

Food holds relational meaning to me. *(connecting, intimate, nurturance, familial, obligation)*	
Yes	*No*

I'm ok with sharing my food with others.	
Yes	*No*

Preparing and cooking for others feels good.		
Rarely	*Sometimes*	*Often*

I'm fine with eating or drinking after someone I'm close to.	
Yes	*No*

Leftovers are just fine with me.	
Yes	*No*

I would describe my relationship with food as:

Spiritual

Spiritual boundaries encompass your personal beliefs, spiritual practices, words or phrases you use to refer to your spirituality, your understanding of a Higher Power, worship practices, your tolerance for different beliefs and practices, etc.

My spiritual beliefs include:
1.
2.
3.
4.
5.

Spiritually, I'm uncomfortable with:
1.
2.
3.
4.
5.

Congratulations! That is quite a comprehensive list you have just covered. You may recognize, some categories hold more energy or are more challenging than others. It's important to review these periodically, especially when conflict arises or there is an internal struggle. Take a breath. That was great work!

Chapter 17

Change Back

"If someone throws a fit because you set boundaries, it's just more evidence the boundary is needed."
~ Unknown

Fairytales, romance novels, and idealized movies cause people to begin romanticizing and sensationalizing relationships. They begin to believe someone will rescue them from their inner aches. With every ticket sold, the expectations soar. In the end, people are set up for tragically unrealistic expectations. Many tend to think their *happily ever after* will finally arrive from outside forces.

Newsflash: There is not a boundary fairy; so, if you're looking for a quick, easy answer, Siri can't even help you this time. If you type *boundaries* into the search bar on Google, you'll get 748,000,000 results. There's a lot to know when navigating boundaries, with no magical guide offering answers.

Knowing how to set, clarify, maintain, and reinforce your boundaries may take practice. Learning how to respond to difficult situations, rather than react, is imperative. Your boundaries should require no convincing or justifying; instead, only your willingness to follow through.

Helping my clients determine their needs is often like specialized detective work. When I ask a client, “What do you need in this situation?” most respond, “I don’t know.” If you don’t know what your preferences and needs are, how do you expect others to know? Listening to outside voices and pleasing and performing for years, lands you in confusion. Point blank, you may have set yourself up for a lifetime of unmet expectations, if not corrected.

People don’t magically know what you want and need. It doesn’t matter how long you’ve known someone or how much they love you, he or she cannot read your mind; and most people suck at guesswork. Take the detective work out of your relationships by being clear about your preferences. The responsibility is yours and has nothing to do with love, romance, or mattering.

Granting yourself permission to have and legitimize needs are important. The more you educate yourself about your needs, the more empowered you’ll be to communicate them. Once you can communicate them, you can use them to establish your boundaries.

People will hear and respect your limits, or they won’t. They’re willing and capable of meeting your needs, or they’re not. It hurts when they can’t, or won’t, but it shows you the truth about them, not you. Trying to force, explain, convince, orchestrate, manipulate, or rage to get your needs met from someone is a losing battle.

Pay attention to what people show you; they'll let you know what you can expect from them. You don't have to like it, but you do need to decide how you'll respond. Expecting more from them is nothing more than naïve, silly, and self-sabotage. Thinking you can plead, reason, or guilt them into hearing you is destructive; and you deserve more than that for goodness sake.

When people disrespect your limits, and you find yourself pleading for the third or hundredth time, listen to them! They're showing you the truth about who they are and what you can expect from them. Continuing to work to get your needs met from someone who has proven themselves unreliable is self-neglect. Yes, you may succumb to disappointment and may be faced with tough choices, but it is still your responsibility to act in your best interest.

Healthy boundaries must be communicated and enforced with intentions to follow through. If you communicate your limits, but aren't prepared to follow through, it's nothing more than a threat. A boundary isn't effective without a consequence. These consequences aren't punishments or attempts to control; they're simply the result of someone's inappropriate behavior that you're willing to act upon.

Do you know the staying power of a three-year-old? Have you ever watched a parent become exacerbated by the sheer will of a toddler? Anyone who has parented effectively has reached the point of waving the white flag as they wander off into a parenting daze. Those small creatures can wear parents down!

Setting boundaries requires the same type of staying power needed when dealing with a stubborn child. Remaining determined and steadfast in the face of a tantrum-throwing person can feel exhausting, defeating, and pointless. It may seem like your boundaries aren't working or like you have *no choice.* Stay the course!

Just like the parent who gives in by handing over the once forbidden lollipop, the moment you cave is the moment you must start all over. If you hold strong through 100 desperate pleas and belligerent demands, but you concede at 101, others now know your breaking point — the line they need to push to get you to cave.

Staying power sucks and it's exhausting; but on the other side is that magical moment when people know you mean business. Then, finally, you begin to matter, because they know they won't be able to change your mind... no matter what.

Throughout your life, you've clearly taught people what to expect from you. They've become accustomed to your reactions, responses, and overall conduct. They know what you'll accept, and what you won't. They know when you mean business, and when you're just sounding the sirens. As you start changing your dance with people, it may get a little messy. You may step on some toes, and they may step on yours; but hopefully, as you commit to the steadfast nature of this work, people will adjust to your new steps.

Sadly, some folks may never adapt, and the dance may be over with them. Either way, determine your staying power as you claim responsibility for the health of your new life. Start small and build your boundaries steadily and firmly.

When you get serious about taking better care of yourself, you'll notice your words, behaviors, and decisions change. There's a clarified energy that ignites within you. Some people won't like it very much, but it's vital for you stay the course. Circumstances may get worse before they get better. This process can be hard, confusing, lonely, and downright torturous at times. However, the reality is, if boundaries were easy to set and enforce, we'd all be living much happier lives.

Clients sometimes say, "I tried setting boundaries, and they just don't work." Once again, I find myself calling, *bullshit*. Through investigating, it's not that the boundaries don't work; rather, people tend to be inconsistent in their assertion of their boundaries. More than likely, they cave before the boundary could become the new norm. If you're not ready to walk the walk of boundaries, people will know it.

I've also heard people say they had no choice in the matter. Let's be clear, you will very rarely have *no choice*. If there are true safety issues at hand, that of course, is a different matter. However, most people feel they have *no choice* when, in reality, the choice is hard with uncomfortable emotions, such as consequences, difficult outcomes, fear, uncertainty, guilt, or conflict. Let's be clear, uncomfortable emotions does not equate to *no choice*. What you really have is a terrible choice A and a terrible choice B.

Have you ever felt like someone is completely on your side as your greatest cheerleader? Even to the extent they encourage you to set limits to take better care of yourself. Then, somehow, when you start to change, they become angry and resistant. Welcome to *Change Back*!

In theory, most people will encourage you to set boundaries and take great care of yourself; however, their tune may change when you become less accommodating. This is because it worked very well for them when you had poor boundaries. Now that they don't always get their way, they feel disturbed, making you feel like there's something wrong with you. Their behavior may escalate to get you to change back because the old ways were far more comfortable for them, even though it wasn't for you.

It is inevitable, you will stumble upon hardships as you begin to set and enforce boundaries. Your emotions will seem unstable, and you may consider waving your white flag. However, once you *find the sweet spot*, setting and enforcing boundaries will come more natural to you. In the next chapter, you will discover the difference between water words and weapon words, to help you find your sweet spot.

www.AllysonBlythe.com

Chapter 18

Water & Weapon Words

"We cannot simultaneously set a boundary and take care of another person's feelings."
~ Melody Beattie

Do you remember the childhood character Goldilocks? Do you recall how some things were a little too much and other things weren't quite enough? Do you remember how everything had to be *just right*? She is a great example of working to get boundaries perfected. Sometimes you may go a little too far, and other times not quite far enough. There is an art to getting boundaries *just right*.

When you first begin practicing boundaries, you may swing all the way from one side to the other of the *approach pendulum*. Meaning, you may be a little too soft or way too tough. It's okay to stumble a bit as you figure out how to get your boundaries *just right*.

As you venture on your boundary setting and enforcing journey, be aware of the following two sides of the approach pendulum.

Water Words

This pattern involves using specific words or phrases that dilute your message. Maybe you feel like you should soften the blow, so you use terms that water down your message in attempt to make it more acceptable. Maybe you're worried about coming off too strong, like bossy or an ass. While using *water words* may reduce the impact, it also weakens your message.

Perhaps you've heard watered down words when a parent asks, "Johnny, we're leaving in five minutes, *okay*?" It implies that Poor Johnny has a voice in the matter because he was asked, not informed. When Johnny doesn't comply or raises a fuss, he's the one in trouble or labeled as *bad*. A healthy parent will advocate, instruct, and redirect. Never ask; unless, it truly is a question.

Watering down your words is typically nothing more than *going along to get along*. It is an attempt at politeness and a plea for approval. It's a means to seem nice, cooperative, and congenial, all while still trying to get others to comply. Water words also indicate a willingness to be flexible. Adding *okay* to your sentence implies you're looking for the other person's permission. It's a mere request, rather than informing someone of your decision. Lose the okay if you're not asking! Stick to your guns!

Not having strong boundaries is like trying to keep a burglar out with a screen door. If your energy is weak, people will know it. So, be sure your boundaries are communicated clearly, respectfully, and directly, with no wiggle room. Make your boundaries known to others, along with the consequences of crossing the line.

Watch for water words such as:

- Okay?
- If you don't mind...
- Do you mind...
- Is it okay if...
- If it's not a bother...
- What if we...
- What if I...
- What if you...
- I prefer...
- I would rather...
- I really don't like that, but...
- How about...

Weapon Words

Weapon Words are on the on the other side of the approach pendulum—they are *fightin' words*. They evoke hostility, threat, and defensiveness, and are not effective at communicating what you want.

These types of words tend to be rigid and defensive. Often, they ignite from someplace very heated and biased, such as your history, old wounds, and unresolved pain. They can be layered with intense emotion, sarcasm, threats, extremes, and blame. Weapon words stem from emotion, rather than a rational response. They discredit you, your word, and potentially your character. Even more, they leave no room for clarity, nor conversation. The biggest risk is, they often make a bad situation worse.

Watch for weapon words such as:

- You can't do that.
- You'd better...
- That will never happen.
- I will never do that.
- You have to...
- What the heck is wrong with you?
- I'm not putting up with your crap anymore.
- There's something wrong with you.
- What's your problem?
- You can't treat me like that.
- That's not true at all.
- You better not ever do that again.

I tend to use...	
Water Words	*Weapon Words*
Some issues I have watered down are:	
1.	
2.	
3.	

Some water words I use are:	

I have used weapon words in these situations:
1.
2.
3.

Some weapon words I use are:	

Hopefully, you are now mindful about swinging from one side of the approach pendulum to the other. It is vital to your success to balance your responses. When you find your *sweet spot* for responding and setting boundaries, enforcing them will become more natural. In the next chapter, you will learn about *finding the sweet spot* to get your responses *just right.*

www.AllysonBlythe.com

Chapter 19

Finding the Sweet Spot

"William James said, 'You cannot travel without until you have travelled within.' Socrates said, "The unexamined life is not worth living.' People who discover their sweet spot are people who take the inward journey and examine themselves. They make the choice to live until they die."

~ Scott M. Fay

Once you begin this practice, you may find yourself swinging wildly from one side of the spectrum to the other. You may bounce back and forth between being passive and aggressive as you struggle to find that sweet spot of assertion. As normal as this is, you may need some direction and clarification about how to find that middle ground in setting your boundaries. In this chapter, we will cover extreme, hostile, and sarcastic responses. Also, you will be spending much of this chapter practicing your response to a variety of scenarios given to you. Let's get started!

Extreme Responses

Extreme responses push too far out along the edges. They're rigid, black and white, all or none responses, such as *always and never.* They rarely portray things accurately, nor get your point across effectively. When you tell someone they *always* do something, they'll think of the one time they didn't. When you tell someone they *never* do something, they'll think of the one time they did. The use of these extremes reflects your pain and frustration but create defensiveness. Also, they don't accurately portray your deepest concerns, and they elude to exaggeration and your discrediting.

Hostile Responses

Threats and accusations are another risky category to be aware of. Flying off the handle, demanding things you can't control, and threatening without follow-through, are examples of hostile responses; and are also an additional category of weapon words.

Cussing, animation, assumptions, intimidation, assigning motives, and personalizing, are patterns that get you caught up in dangerous thinking. Also, they make you ineffective at dealing with the actual issue at hand. The first sign of these is evidence of the need for a boundary.

Sarcastic Responses

Small disclaimer... I love sarcasm! I think it's funny, witty, and clever. However, I also know it can be a passive aggressive way to poke at someone under the guise of humor. Then, when the other person gets upset, it's easy to turn it back on them as if they're too sensitive and can't take a joke.

The Latin definition of sarcasm is *the tearing of flesh.* I encourage you to consider your audience and your honest motive before letting sarcasm fly. It may be a very passive way you are trying to make a point, but sarcasm is also a category of weapon words.

The following childhood adage is important to note here: *Say what you mean. Mean what you say. Don't say it mean.*

Take a moment to think back to the Goldilocks story so you can begin practicing communicating your boundaries *just right.*

Example #1
A friend is having a 40th birthday dinner next Thursday. She has asked you to attend and to be the Designated Driver for her special event. You are excited to celebrate and honor your friend. However, you also realize the next morning is the team meeting where you will be delivering the annual presentation. Though you wrestle with the competing situations, you know both events are important, so you want to find a way to partake in both.

A week before her birthday, you have a conversation with your friend about the evening and your needs and limits—you're willing to drive, but you must leave the dinner by 9:00 pm. This way you can be well-rested for your meeting in the morning. She, of course, is welcome to stay past 9:00, but will need to arrange for another ride home if she chooses to do stay later. She agrees, appearing grateful for the ride, and in full agreement for a great night out ending by 9:00 p.m.

The night arrives and seems to be going well. As 8:50 p.m. rolls around, you begin to gather your things. At the same time, your friend asks the waiter for another drink. You inquire, "I'll be leaving in just a few minutes, so will you be getting another ride home?" She asks you to stay a bit longer, and you remind her that it's 9:00, and that you're leaving. She gets really angry and proceeds to tell you that you're a terrible friend and you always ruin things.

Your heart sinks, disappointed that the evening turned this way, as you realize you have a situation on your hands. You recognize the dilemma and understand the importance of the situation in front of you, so you muster the strength to address it with her. However, even as you're speaking, you realize your message is filled with watered down words.

"Hey, listen, I really have to leave at 9:00, okay?
I don't mean to ruin your night. I hope it's okay, but I
have to go. I'm really sorry. I'll stay for 15 more
minutes, but then I'm going to need to go.
I'm sorry about the inconvenience."

She sits, staring blankly at her drink and doesn't appear to be budging anytime soon. The fury begins to boil inside of you. You grab ahold of your imaginary boundary rope to find yourself swinging all the way to the other side, where you begin blasting your weapon words.

"You are so damn selfish!
I should've known this would happen.
Seriously?! You're going to act like this?
I swear I will never do anything nice
for you ever again."

Then, you storm out of the place, sticking her with your bill, determined to never speak to her again.

Yikes! No sweet spot there. Let's get some help from *good ole' Goldie* to see if she can help define a sweet spot with these boundaries.

At 8:50 p.m., your friend orders another drink and you calmly reinforce your previously agreed upon plan to leave by 9:00 p.m. She nods as she continues to sit, drinking and chatting with the others, seemingly angry that you plan to leave. You wave your goodbyes and head out for the night promptly at 9:00 p.m. It's okay that she's angry, you didn't do anything wrong. You communicated ahead of time, clarified, and followed through. There is no sense rehashing or bashing... Ba... Da... Bing! Goldilocks has your gold star waiting!

Having made the boundary clear long before the event, enables you to stand firm. It also allows your friend to make whatever choice she wants to make; and she's responsible for that choice. You communicated the plan, and she originally agreed. She, of course, is free to change her mind, and you are free to follow through. Trying to force her to leave or staying longer than you want are unhealthy behaviors that are attempts to control or subjugate, which both lead to nowhere good.

Example #2

You notice the evening news is causing you stress and draining your energy by the end of the day. You begin to dream of a quiet evening without the noise of the television. Your partner is a political junkie and thrives on the news feed. You can feel your signs and symptoms beginning to brew, so you know it's time for another plan.

Your first attempt is filled with watered down words, such as:

> "Hey, if it's not too much trouble, I'd rather not watch the news tonight. Do you mind if we watch something else? I don't mean to be a pain, but I need a break. It's starting to bother me."

That response is oozing with passivity and is an indirect way to get the person to hear you and cooperate. With no response from your partner, you reach your breaking point and are now making that wild swing, slinging weapon words.

> "I swear, if I walk in here one more time and hear the news, I'm going to tear that tv off

the wall. How about you show me half as much attention as you show that damn tv?"

You hide the remote and swear there must have been a break-in earlier that day.

Goldilocks To The Rescue:

"I'm not interested in the news. I'd prefer to turn it off, but if it's important to you, I'll head downstairs for now. I'm going to go for a walk later. Do you want to join me?"

Remember, people will show you who they are and what you can expect from them. Pay attention because it will offer you some truth about the relationship. If your needs and requests consistently go unmet or ignored, pay attention to what the person is showing you, even if it leaves you with tough choices.

Here are a few more examples of the Goldilocks sweet spot.

> Someone is really upset and cussing at you. You respond "That language bothers me. If you speak to me like that again, I'm going to hang up the phone." Then, if it continues, you hang up the phone.
>
> ...
>
> A customer calls at 7:00 p.m., two hours after your business has closed. During the call, the next day, you reinforce your hours of business.

"I'm available until 5:00 p.m. Anything after hours will get my full attention the next day. How can I be of assistance to you now?"

...

A friend asks to borrow $200. This is a friend who has borrowed from you in the past, but never repaid. "I hear what a jam you're in and I'm not able to help with any finances. I'm happy to cook dinner on Friday if you'd like to come over." (The last part is offered only if you have it to give.)

You can firmly, lovingly, and directly say what you mean, without the wild swing of being too passive or aggressive. You deserve to speak your truth, and people deserve to hear it to maintain a healthy relationship.

Let's hand over the keys so you can give it a test run. Below are a few more Goldilocks opportunities for you to try.

You're on a third date with someone you like, and you are interested in getting to know this person more. The attraction is high, the drinks were many, and the chemistry is flowing. However, you are certain it's time to call an Uber. As you proceed to tell him or her you need to leave, they insist you come over to *sleep it off*.

Your response:

Your mother-in-law stops by unannounced, despite years of requesting she call first.

Your response:

Your kid sister is a mother of two, unemployed, and called to complain about her eviction notice.

Your response:

The previous exercise was a test! How'd you do? Notice it simply stated *she called to complain.* Did you offer input, solutions, or assistance when she didn't ask for it? Just checking...

> Your kid sister is a mother of two, unemployed, and called to complain about her eviction notice. During the call, she asked if she and the kids can move in with you.

Your response:

Notice the difference in the above two examples? The only change is that now has she asked for your help. It doesn't mean your answer needs to change, at all. Remember, if boundaries were easy, we'd all be setting them!

What are some blanket *Goldilocks* responses you can offer in a variety of situations?
1.
2.
3.
4.
5.

Chapter 20

Vibe

"To know thy self is the beginning of wisdom."
~ Socrates

The process to proclaim your authenticity is transformative; a journey of becoming. Learning to show up in life without false representations is one of the most empowering, attractive, alluring acts you can do. Also, it allows people to truly know your deepest, truest self. Powerful, yet scary!

The emotional energy you carry is very real. People can sense your vibe by your tonality, eye contact, posture, and the overall way you carry yourself. Early in my career when I did sex offender treatment work, one individual clearly told me, "I know within minutes of meeting someone if I can offend them or not. It may take me a while to figure out how to do it, but I know whether or not I can, just by the way they act and hold their body." ***Bone-chilling...***

Have you ever instantly not liked someone? They walk into a room and you just hate their guts? Those feelings you have are the same concept as what my client was saying. It's important to recognize the energy you carry and the message it portrays. The way you represent yourself matters, not to please or perform, but to ensure your genuine truth. This sets you up to lead life from the inside out.

The way you relate to others interactively is equally important. The way you converse, connect, and offer says a lot about your inner working. Some people carry hard, piercing energy that is blocking, angry, or defensive, which attracts or repels certain types of people. You may also present yourself as cold, distant, aloof, hardened, or disinterested. Perhaps you bring in heavy emotions with depth and despair. Maybe there's even intensity, chaos, or drama surrounding the way you show up. It's not right or wrong, but it's another critical point of awareness.

Some people are a bit more eager in relationships, and present a clutching, clinging energy. Certainly, they're nice and helpful, but something is off. Though this eagerness may be intended to connect to people, it often has the opposite effect. From the outside, people can sense that far reaching, latching energy, and actually feel repelled by it. Behavior like this tends to be attention and approval seeking; perhaps, even based on old wounds and unmet needs, as though they are trying to fill a void.

Are you someone who really *leans forward* in relationships with overly eager, seeking energy? Do you try too hard to get people to like you or make an impression on them? Are you longing for connection or to fill an ache or need? Have you been trying extremely hard with good-hearted intentions, but find people don't respond to you? Well-intended energy, such as this, energetically drives people away and is sabotaging to real, healthy connections.

If there are consistent patterns with the type of people you attract (the results you get from your relationships), you may want to consider checking your vibe. Take note if you need to adjust for improved patterns of relating and engaging.

My client, Claire, sat in front of me, perched on the edge of the couch. Seven months prior, she had been diagnosed with depression and precisely followed the doctor's recommendations, with no relief to her symptoms. "I just don't understand," she spoke slowly trying to hold back her tears. "I'm really a good person. I just don't understand why things always end up this way. I try to get people to like me. I'm kind, thoughtful, and am always the first one to help. Why is it that no one seems to care about me the way I care about them?"

No doubt Claire was sad; perhaps even depressed. She needed some serious intervention. But, medication? There is no pill to help with this problem. Claire had a serious case of TTH (*Trying Too Hard*).

Claire presented herself as very eager and accommodating, leaning far forward with high energy to reach people. She left little to no room for others to do any of the engaging work. Her self-esteem and value were placed in their hands, and when they didn't respond or reciprocate, she was paralyzed by despair. Claire's constant attempts to *get* people to like her, were perhaps the exact reasons they didn't.

Let's see if you have a case of TTH.

It's important that people like me.		
Not at All	*Somewhat*	*Incredibly*

I find myself trying hard to make connections with others.		
Rarely	*Sometimes*	*Often*

I'm impacted by the way people respond to me.		
Not at All	*Somewhat*	*Incredibly*

I think I lean too far forward (eagerness) in relationships when I'm trying to connect.		
Rarely	*Sometimes*	*Often*

What other people think of me matters.		
Not at All	*Somewhat*	*Incredibly*

The words I would use to describe my energy are:	

In the next chapter, you will discover seven more energy types that could be sabotaging your relationships, even if your heart is the purest of all hearts. We will go over the 7 M's: Mothering, Monitoring, Managing, Meddling, Manipulating, Martyrdom, Moping, and they will provide you with insight into the well-intended patterns you may be using to connect.

www.AllysonBlythe.com

Chapter 21

The 7 M's

"Let people do what they need to do to make them happy: Mind your own business and do what you need to do to make you happy."

~ Leon Brown

THE 7 M'S	
Mothering	**Monitoring**
Managing	**Meddling**
Manipulating	**Martyrdom**
Moping	

It's fascinating what happens when you start being honest with yourself. As you explore your motives, you begin noticing what you're doing and why you're doing it. Then, your entire outlook changes. The following is a list of patterns and energies in which you may be using when engaging with people. Take your time with this chapter and consider each pattern carefully.

Mothering

Mothering patterns stem from your attempts to care for others; nurture someone. It is energy that puts you in the caretaking and protective position and authorizes you as the decision maker and the one who knows best. For a five or twelve-year-old, these patterns are necessary and appropriate. Not so much with adults. This is parental energy that erodes another person's dignity.

Mothering encompasses offering correction, input, direction, and suggestions to someone without being asked. It includes doing things for others that they're capable of doing for themselves, catering to people, and not allowing adults to be responsible for their actions, decisions, and consequences. Even more, it is expecting others to *fall into [your] line*.

Scott is 37, and his wife Sarah is 34. Every morning before Scott went to work, Sarah laid out his clothes for him, including socks and underwear, and ensuring his clothes matched and were neatly pressed. She would check his appearance before he left the house each morning. When pressed for clarification, Sarah reported that it was her duty to make sure he looked presentable so his coworkers would know how well she was taking care of him. On the other hand, Sarah was baffled why Scott seemed incapable of basic chores such as taking out the trash or putting away his neatly laundered clothing once a week.

I tend to take care of people and feel responsible for them.		
Rarely	*Sometimes*	*Often*

What other people do and say is a reflection of me.		
Rarely	*Sometimes*	*Often*

Three people I try to mother are:
1.
2.
3.

Three mothering behaviors I've used are:
1.
2.
3.

Monitoring

As an adult, it can be challenging to keep track of yourself. Yet, someone who monitors tends to mind other people's business more than their own. This pattern encompasses observing another person to assess what you think they should or shouldn't be doing.

Monitoring includes checking up on or checking in on someone, gauging another's mood, status, behavior, and decisions, and making sure they stay in alignment with a course you approve.

Joy smoked when she met Jeff. Jeff fell deeply in love with Joy, but equally despised her *disgusting habit,* as he called it. Every day Jeff would track the number of cigarettes Joy smoked. Though Joy really did have a desire to quit, she reported that her smoking had actually increased since she met Jeff.

I want people to change.		
Rarely	*Sometimes*	*Often*

People, places, or things I monitor are:	

I monitor because...

Managing

Managing encompasses supervising, advising, dictating, and asserting authority. It puts you in control of someone else as though you are responsible for the results of their life. Managers tend to regulate the *right way* things should be done with rules, procedures, and routines; and they have the final say.

Liz grew up in a military home that was run like clockwork, and no one would dare challenge the rigid expectations and routine. Her father had a say in every last detail of her life, including the clothes she wore, the boy she went to the Senior Prom with, and the college she attended. At 27, Liz felt incapable of deciding on her own without consulting the opinions of others, and her father's opinion always outweighed her own.

It's important for me to manage things in my home.		
Rarely	*Sometimes*	*Often*

It's important to me that people do what I think needs to be done.		
Rarely	*Sometimes*	*Often*

There's usually a right way to do things. My way.		
Rarely	*Sometimes*	*Often*

Managing people and situations helps me feel or prevents me from feeling these emotions:	

Meddling

Meddling encompasses getting involved in other people's business, interfering, inserting your opinion, and occupying yourself in people's affairs without their request or permission. Butting into someone else's life can look like a lot of different things: telling someone what they should or shouldn't be doing, gossip, offering your opinion without being asked, snooping, or otherwise interfering.

Maria's daughter, Alicia came to visit every week. During each visit, Maria would endlessly inquire about Alicia's dating life, comment about the way she was styling her hair and the makeup she wore, and never seemed to miss an opportunity to make remarks about the Alicia's weight.

When her daughter excused herself from the dinner table to use the restroom, Maria felt it was the prime opportunity to go through Alicia's purse. She was mortified to find prescription medication safely tucked in a pouch. Maria was confused and furious that her daughter wouldn't come to her with her problems and tell her about the medicine.

I want to know what's going on in other people's lives.		
Rarely	*Sometimes*	*Often*

I tend to know what's best for someone I care about.		
Rarely	*Sometimes*	*Often*

It's my responsibility to offer input and suggestions, even if someone hasn't asked.		
Rarely	*Sometimes*	*Often*

I find myself meddling in other people's business.		
Rarely	*Sometimes*	*Often*

I do this because...

Manipulating

This is a sneaky pattern and is often subtle or seemingly innocent that it goes unrecognized. Manipulating encompasses trying to orchestrate circumstances, outcomes, or people to do or not do something. These are attempts to influence people, places, or things to create a certain outcome.

Ivan was in the dating world, ready to marry and start a family over the next several years. His family was eager to meet the next generation of children and thought it would be helpful to start introducing Ivan to more people to help him find the love of his life.

Suddenly, his social calendar began filling with oddly arranged family dinner meetings, neighborhood parties, and drink nights with nice, attractive strangers his family thought he should meet. Ivan was shocked and infuriated when he started to get emails from women who had seen his dating profile; a dating profile he did not create.

It troubles me when things don't work out the way I want them to.		
Rarely	*Sometimes*	*Often*

I have good ideas about what other people should be doing.		
Rarely	*Sometimes*	*Often*

I resort to nagging, criticizing, and complaining to get people to do things.		
Rarely	*Sometimes*	*Often*

I have a lot of concern for people and feel obligated to help and work things out for them.		
Rarely	*Sometimes*	*Often*

If people would listen to my ideas, their life would work out better.		
Rarely	*Sometimes*	*Often*

Martyrdom

Martyrdom encompasses exaggerated suffering that is often an attempt to get attention, sympathy, support, love, and understanding; but the distress is done at your own hand. These patterns are filled with constant long suffering, sacrifice, victimhood, and lament.

Martyrdom is playing the victim and believing you have no choice in matters. It is self-induced suffering and being overly responsible for others while not accepting responsibility for yourself.

It was 3:00 a.m. when Alma finally fell into bed. She was exhausted from running all day, picking up, sorting, tidying, mending, getting the soccer bags ready, packing lunches, and making the grocery list; there was just so much to do for her teen children.

The next day she flew out of bed raging and crying about how unappreciated she was, how lazy and irresponsible her kids were, and how much they are going to miss her when she dies. Alma was now late for an 8:30 meeting she had with her boss. She felt struck when her eighteen-year-old son said, “Well, I guess you should’ve just gone to bed.” It was a harsh reality that no one would ever understand or appreciate the sacrifices she makes.

I am exhausted by the needs and irresponsibility of others.		
Rarely	*Sometimes*	*Often*

There is always so much to do, it's hard for me to rest and prioritize my needs.		
Rarely	*Sometimes*	*Often*

I make sacrifices and work hard, at my own expense.		
Rarely	*Sometimes*	*Often*

A little acknowledgment and appreciation would go a long way for me.		
Rarely	*Sometimes*	*Often*

Moping

Shall I introduce you to Eeyore? Eeyore is quite a creature filled with heavy, depressed, apathetic energy that he carries into all his affairs. He is a glass half empty kind of dude; and if something is going to go wrong, Eeyore has already thought about it, played it out, and surrendered to it.

Moping encompasses heavy, sad, and depressed energy that influences the way you see and approach situations, and the way people perceive you. It is apathetic or dejected, and can dim hope, positivity, and connection.

Shanelle had gotten a raise at work, been asked out by the guy she had been interested in for months, got the last Danish pastry on the shelf, hit all the green lights on the way to work, and just scratched off a $50 lottery ticket. When she walked into the office her coworker greeted her and questioned, "What's wrong, you look upset?" Shanelle proceed to complain about the increased taxes she was going to have to pay, the powdered sugar she had gotten on her shirt, the long drive to a date tonight, and the predetermined outcome that this guy wasn't really interested in her anyway. Her coworker was dazed by the blast of negativity, shrugged as she walked away, stammering "Well, good luck, I guess."

I see the glass as:	
Half Empty	*Half Full*

I tend to focus on the things that could go wrong in life.		
Rarely	*Sometimes*	*Often*

It's hard for me to remain positive or trust that things will go well.		
Rarely	*Sometimes*	*Often*

Each of the seven patterns are strategies you have been using to try to get different needs met. Though counterproductive and ineffective, they are ways you have learned to relate and offer love and support. Perhaps you haven't even recognized the toll they've taken on you and on others.

Below is a chart with each of the seven M's. In this chart, you will see a brief reminder about each of their behaviors. In the space provided on the right side of the chart, write in what needs you are seeking to meet by embracing the behaviors.

Pattern	Behavior	Your Needs
Mothering	**Parental Energy:** Nurturing. Caretaker. Protective. Decision Maker. Correcting. Suggestions. Responsible.	
Monitoring	**Regulator Energy:** Checking up on. Checking in on. Gauging mood, status, behavior, and decisions.	
Managing	**Liable Energy:** Supervising. Advising. Dictating. Asserting authority.	

Meddling	**Invasion Energy:** Interfering. Butting In. Inserting. Occupying. Gossiping. Snooping.	
Manipulating	**Governor Energy:** Orchestrate. Influence. Control the outcome.	
Martyrdom	**Emotional Energy:** Exaggerating. Long-suffering. Sacrifice. Victimhood. Lament.	
Moping	**Dimming Energy:** Glass half empty. Fearful. Negative. Pity Party. Worse case scenario.	

Learning to recognize the energy you carry, being honest about your motives, and understanding the ways you engage with others can be eye-opening, shocking, and overwhelming.

What if you had to wear your energy as a badge pinned on your shirt to inform people what they're about to get involved with? Would you feel embarrassed, ashamed, or worried? Would you consider things a bit more carefully? Though these behaviors are understandable, given you are merely trying to fulfill a need, you should not be embarrassed or ashamed. The truth is, you do wear these patterns wherever you go. No, they are not displayed or pinned on your shirt; but, remember, people do sense and feel your energy… it's just unspoken.

Indeed, I believe, you are well-intended with the use of the seven behaviors. However, there's a clear overstep that robs others of their dignity. Even more, they burden and overwhelm you, while taxing your relationships. Any use of these behaviors is evidence of codependent, dysfunctional relationships.

As longstanding, loving, and protective as these patterns may seem, they aren't loving. Instead, they are attempts to enforce your will, to prevent or create certain outcomes, to manage consequences, and to impact you or your loved one. In other words, they are attempts to play God, if you will.

Your behaviors may be subtle, with every intention to influence and guide someone you really care about. You may feel guilt, obligation, confusion, and worry if you don't engage in these ways because, to you, they feel like love. Perhaps you have grave concern about the direction of someone else's life and feel as though you *must* get involved.

Moving forward, it's important to know that these patterns are counterproductive to healthy love and connection. They will serve as warning signs to healthy people and are likely to send them packing. Everyone seeking nourishing connection wants to be accepted, heard, and understood; not changed, fixed, or told what to do.

Your willingness to see and own the part you play in relationships, will change the course of how you relate. Taking a good, hard look at how you've added to the dysfunction can feel like unraveling everything you've ever known. However, it's really handing you the keys to awareness, responsibility, and personal choice.

Focusing on how others have hurt you and finding fault in them, may come naturally, especially knowing how loving or innocent your intentions are. Yet, buying into this type of thinking will get you a one-way ticket to a victim fest because you can't control other people. That train ride ends here. As an adult, you have a personal responsibility to yourself; whether you see it, feel it, and believe it, or not.

You may have been spending a lot of time, energy, and effort working to get people to change, to get through to or reason with them, and make them understand your point. Trying to force other people to hear you, convincing them to change, focusing on their behaviors, and engaging in emotional battles are ways you dismiss your own personal power and responsibility. If you're unhappy in a situation, it is crucial to look at the part *you're* playing in it, so you can change. Now that you see your patterns and understand the needs you have been trying to fulfill, you have a starting point to get your eyes off other people and onto yourself.

You can't read the label from inside the bottle. Learning to recognize your own behavior can be like that. As you let go of excuses and justifications, you'll understand the impact you've had on yourself, and others, and become aware of your old patterns. It's okay if it takes time. This can be especially difficult to digest because, indeed, you were doing the best you could, and didn't understand how much you were working against yourself while adding to the problem.

New ways of engaging will take practice and a firm decision made to behave differently, regardless of the consequences. It's a readiness and a mindset.

In the next chapter, you will discover some new terms and conditions for engaging with others. The old script that was written, no longer applies here. Let's get started looking at some new guidelines.

Chapter 22

To Give or Not to Give

"No one has ever become poor by giving."
~ Anne Frank

"Those who are happiest are
those who do the most for others."
~ Booker T. Washington

Will the world rattle if I call bullshit on quotes like the ones above? Sadly, I think it's unequivocal statements like these that cause confusion and shame. Certainly, there's a time and place for inspiration and motivation like this; but too much is really too much. Constant giving causes people to feel the toxic pressure to pour from an empty cup. Unconditional, blanketed statements like these are misleading and detrimental.

As you come to terms with your old patterns and dive deeply into understanding, you may find yourself bewildered as to what to do and not do. Also, you may question whether to get involved with someone or something. You may be asking, "So, now what?"

Decide for yourself to stand in the new, unfamiliar place of apprehension as you make the commitment to stay the course. Listening to and following your inner voice is the best place to begin. Yes, it takes practice; yes, you will be afraid; yes, relationships will change; yes, you will endure some difficulties. Brace yourself for the journey as you learn to tune into your inner voice.

We don't always need a cinder block upside the head to learn a lesson and see the truth about a person or situation. Sometimes, we clearly know that someone or something is bad news. Other times, you're uncertain or doubting yourself because it's not so clear. Having some external guidelines may be helpful in the process of making decisions.

In this chapter, I'll give you some terms and conditions for giving, developing your standards, and maintaining awareness to help you understand that generosity has limits. Take what you like and leave the rest. The following guidelines suggest a framework to better care for yourself, better relate to others, and empowerment through monitored generosity. This way you cultivate a world that promotes wholesome giving, with love and permission to enter yourself at the top of the list.

The goal of this is not to turn you into a selfish, self-absorbed asshole. The world is desperate for kindness and generosity, and there is a middle ground. The goal is to turn the tide on your giving, so you are capable of wholesome, gratified relationships in which giving becomes the natural order, while keeping your soul full.

"There was such a thing as giving too much after all."
~ Justin Somper

Every vehicle is equipped with a visible fuel gauge that reflects vital information to the driver. Clearly, you know you can only journey so far before needing to refuel. The gauge is easy to read and is respected as a valid measuring tool that keeps you from serious consequences.

The truth is, you also have an imaginary fuel tank. We've discussed the *low fuel cues* already: fatigue, irritation, weariness, resentment, etc. The issue is, many people have been trained and shamed to ignore, override, and dismiss the cues.

Feelings are energies that call for your attention. Indeed, some emotions are intense and uncomfortable, but there are no wrong feelings. Yes, behaviors can be unhealthy and destructive, but feelings are cues. Rage, hurt, sadness, despair, fear, etc. are all normal, natural signals that are instinctively prompting you to pay attention. Learning to recognize, becoming comfortable with, and honoring your feelings are the most powerful ways you can navigate through life.

Let's briefly revisit your commodities:

- Time
- Energy
- Effort

Monitoring and managing these parts of your life is essential to assess your true capacity for giving in all context. Befriending your internal cues is a great place to start embracing your instinct and intellect to make a collaborative decision between your heart and your head. This level of emotional navigation will empower you to live intentionally.

Imagine if you came with a visible, credible fuel gauge that easily measured the levels of your time, energy, and effort; a tank that got the same respect, understanding, and attention as the one on an automobile. Imagine if you learned at an early age that close consideration and responsiveness to your fuel levels are essential to ensure safe travel with others. Moving forward, it is imperative to gauge your personal fuel tank on each of these valuable resources of time, energy, and effort.

Let's investigate your imaginary fuel tanks. Where would the needle register when measuring your time, energy, and effort? Are you typically someone who runs the tank empty? Do you know when you start to get low and need to refuel?

My top 3 signs of needing to refuel are:
1.
2.
3.

Improving the health of your relationships is a sure way to monitor your tank to keep it as full as possible. The goal is not to end all your relationships, nor to stop giving altogether. However, to create healthy relationships it's crucial to rewrite the guidelines for future engagements.

When deciding to get involved with something or someone, here are some important parameters to consider:

- Have I been asked to help?
  - Many people offer help without being asked to help.
- Do I want to be involved?
- How do I honestly feel about this?
- Do I have the time, energy, and effort to give?
- What's the cost of this to me and my commodities?
- What is my motive for getting involved?
- Have I taken care of my responsibilities first?
- Am I working harder on this than they are?
- Is it in my best interest?
- Am I coming from a place of fear, obligation, guilt, habit, or seeking love?
- Am I trying to control, fix, or rescue?
- Am I trying to force my plan and my will on someone else?

- Am I trying to orchestrate a certain outcome or result?
- What are my expectations or hopes if I do get involved?
- Can I do it for fun and for free, without future demands, expectations, or impositions?
- Is this something they can do themselves?
- Has this become a pattern or habit?
- Have I considered all my choices?
    - Give what you have, rather than their full expectation. Perhaps drive someone to work one time, instead of five times.
- Have they considered all their options outside of me?
    - Can they ask someone else? Can they take the bus? Can they adjust their plans?
- Am I saying *yes* because I'm afraid to say *no*? What am I afraid of?
- Am I prepared to follow through?

Those terms and conditions are the new rules of engagement. Take each one of them into consideration before you say "yes" or "no." Over time, they will become natural as you learn to trust and honor your intuition. In the meantime, use this as your personal checklist to help you determine the *who, what, when, where, how, and why* of getting involved.

You may be well-established in the dysfunctional terrain of relationships. It is habit; and on some level it is also comfortable and familiar. You've grown accustomed to everything you've been taught and trained. Now is the time to decide differently.

"You know, sometimes all you need is 20 seconds of insane courage. Just literally 20 seconds of just embarrassing bravery. And I promise you, something great will come of it."
~ Benjamin Mee, We Bought a Zoo

Imagine a Trapeze Artist, teetering high above safe ground, firmly perched on a tiny landing. With eyes staunchly focused on the other side, the artist takes the final step, swinging wildly into the air, releasing the illusion of safety from the small landing. Enticing and alluring, yet horrifying at the same time.

That's what it can feel like to step into a new way of loving and relating to others. Taking a step away from the familiar can be just as alarming, yet exhilarating. It may feel like a terrifying abyss in which you're certain that with just the slightest misstep, you'll fall to your impending doom. Or, perhaps, you will step into the wildest, riveting ride of your life as you arrive safely and firmly on the other side. That's what vulnerability feels like.

Here's hope...
The brain can stop thinking about something when it

starts thinking about something else. So, instead of thinking about the terrifying step off the platform and the horrifying drop below, think about the victory that awaits you. Below are a few ways to direct your brain to focus on victory, instead of demise.

- Breathe. As simple as it sounds, this is your starting point. The fight or flight part of your brain takes over during stress and conflict. Therefore, you're likely holding your breath or engaging in very shallow breathing. Breathe, breathe again, and then breathe more deeply.
- Visualize sending the emotions down through your body so you're not clinging and clutching the stress of it all. Use your breath to guide your emotions out through your feet and into the earth, rather than holding them inside of you.
- When thoughts begin to flood and you're having a hard time managing your emotions, practice saying a particular word or mantra to give your mind something to grab ahold of. The Serenity Prayer is great for this:

"God, grant me the serenity to accept
the things I cannot change. Change the things
I can. And the wisdom to know the difference."

- Learn to develop and follow through with a *Plan B* so you can enforce your limits. Be willing to take a stand for yourself.
- Pay attention to what life is trying to tell you. You don't have to like it; but listen to the cues life offers you. Struggle and resistance are often signaling that you're working too hard, forcing solutions, or trying to orchestrate life by your terms.
- People will show you who they really are. Pay attention. Again, you don't have to like it, but it's important to see.
- Focus on what adds to your commodities and invest heavily in them.
    - Rest, nature, golf, painting, friends, working out, travel, etc.
- Be flexible without losing yourself. Understand, there is right and wrong in the world, but there's also differences. Know that there are a lot of ways to do things, and your way may not be the only way. Years ago, a good friend had to remind me that there are many ways to get to 8. 4 + 4 might make the most sense to you, but 10 – 2 also leads you there. Everyone must find their own path and you can't decide for them.
- Make friends with your feelings and your fuel gauge. Respect them as valuable cues and

information that are your responsibility to manage.

- Learn to give based on what you have, rather than what others want from you.
- Check your commodities before giving. If it will cost you too much in any area, consider carefully.
- Start with small steps so you can practice. It's okay to begin with simple boundaries to build up your strength.
- Trust your internal GPS: Gut, Perception, Senses. Your mind and body were designed to be listened to and honored.

"Authenticity is the daily practice of letting go of who we think we're supposed to be and embracing who we are."

~ Brené Brown

Chapter 23

The Power of No

"It's only by saying 'no' that you can concentrate on the things that are really important."

~ Steve Jobs

"I refuse to please others at the expense of my emotional well-being. Even if it means saying 'no' to people who are used to hearing 'yes'."

~ Unknown

No. The power and magnitude of one word... the simplicity and ease of it, too... two little letters put together for such profound meaning and significance. The word *no* can be history making, dream crushing, heart shattering, life altering, and yet, just two little letters.

No is, perhaps, one of the easiest words in our language, yet one of the most difficult to utter. Are you riddled with guilt when you say *no*? Do you agonize over the conflict that may stem from saying it? Are you fearful of the consequences when you dare voice the word? Does it feel like gravel in your mouth as you try to find the courage to speak it?

No is a word that holds significant power and meaning. It can evoke defensiveness, hostility, and anger. You may take it very personally and as a rejection or see it as a challenge or as defeat. It can be cruel, harsh, and devastating. Oh, the power it holds...

Newsflash: You can be an incredibly kindhearted, considerate, thoughtful, loving, and supportive person and still use the word *no*. As a matter of fact, the more you use it, the more likely you'll be those descriptions to a greater, deeper, more genuine extent.

The use of the word *no* has been complicated, and many have it misconstrued. It's been used reactively, defensively, limitedly, and indirectly, so the understanding of it is distorted.

There are times that the use of *no* is simplistic. It can equate simply to uttering the words: *end of the story*. No need to overthink, justify, nor explain.

Though I agree that *no* is a complete sentence, I also understand it can be a bit abrasive. Further, most people have the need for understanding. Their questioning may be an attempt to change your mind, but it may also be an attempt to gain understanding for your reasons behind you saying *no*. There's no harm in offering explanation to help someone fully understand your reasons. Clarifying and explaining can help people digest your answer a little easier.

Explanation vs. Justification

Explanations offer facts and relevant information to help someone understand. You can offer details and describe something fully if you want to provide clarity. There are times when a bit more understanding and clarification can help someone digest your *no* answer.

Justification is different. If you're justifying, you're trying to legitimize yourself or your point, as though you must prove your reasons. Justification is an attempt to talk someone out of their feelings, opinions, or reactions because you were *right* in saying *no.*

Let's say you show up at my office on time for your 1:00 appointment and I simply state, "I can't see you right now." and slam the door in your face. Though factual, that approach is also abrasive. Allow me to offer an explanation. You show up, I state, "I cannot see you right now. I have a family emergency and must leave the office." Fair enough; proper explanation. With just a bit more information, you now understand my reason and are fully entitled to kindly accept the change in plans or be upset.

Let's say you are upset about the change in plans. In the face of your response, I start to feel guilty and move into justification, "Listen, I've never done this before, and you need to understand that I have a life too. This is really serious, and you shouldn't be mad. I'll make it up to you. Please don't be upset. I really have to go, and you know I value our time together, but this is an emergency."

Wait... what? Way too much information, layered with

guilt, and unnecessary lament. Life happens and I have a responsibility to myself. You are free to have any response you need to have, without it forcing me to justify.

You can explain a situation and allow room for the other person's reaction. People might be disappointed, upset, surprised, and angry; and that's okay. Their response does not indicate you've done anything wrong. It simply means they are having an emotional reaction to a situation. You can stand firm in your need to handle your circumstances without owning the other person's emotions. You are allowed to say *no* (change plans, etc.) without taking other's emotions personally, nor changing your mind.

Explaining vs. justifying can be a fine line that is important for you to gauge when you're nearing the brink of crossing that line. Too much information, repeating yourself, and a sense of urgency or defense are indicators of justifying.

Creative Ways to Say "No"

A simple *no* may seem too direct at times. Therefore, knowing how to firmly refuse, while softening the blow, may make it easier for you, and them. As you learn to wield the power of this word, I'll encourage you to sit with your feelings and your motives. When used truthfully, purposefully, knowingly, thoughtfully, candidly, firmly, and with respect, this word propels you into intentionality and personal empowerment.

Though just two simple letters, learning to say *no* may take smaller steps before finding comfort in using it. If you have been a *yes person* for a long time or you have disproportionate levels of guilt and ownership, offering a simple *no* can be quite a leap.

Let's play this out in the scenario below.

Fred is a great manager. You've worked for him for years, and you like him a lot. However, recently, he has repeatedly come to you ask you to sit on another volunteer committee. He explains how overwhelmed he is with the tasks he must manage and states he could really use your help. You are annoyed at all the extra efforts, and you recognize how much time you've been spending on these committees. Having carefully considered your options, being certain about your motives, and weighing the cost to your commodities, you've decided the right answer to Fred's request is *no.* You also recognize you care about him, and he is very used to you saying *yes.* You feel a bit wobbly in being able to firmly and confidently state your *no.*

Here are some examples of ways you can creatively decline:

- I'd love to, but I have other commitments that I'm dedicated to.
- I'll have to pass on that.
- My calendar just won't allow me one more commitment right now.

- I'm not my best when I overcommit, so I'm going to say no.
- That sounds great. I'm sorry, I can't help you on this one.
- I'm unable to do that.
- It's not a good fit for me, but thanks for thinking of me. I hope it goes well.
- I can see how much you're struggling. I'm sorry I can't help.
- I'm going to sit this one out.
- I can't help, but I can provide you with some other resources.
- I've learned that less is more for me, so I'm going to decline.
- I'm focusing my time on other things right now.
- That's not my thing.

Fred may be caught off guard, and he may still try to convince you or change your mind. Stand firm. Let Fred have his reaction.

Start Small

When you first practice saying *no* and are trying to assert yourself, start small with strangers, safe people, or with issues that don't matter very much.

- You're out somewhere and someone solicits, "Excuse me ma'am... " You smile, make eye contact, and say, "No thank you." as you keep walking.

- A waitress brings your food that is over cooked. You flag her down and say, "I would like to have this prepared again. This one is far too cooked for my taste."
- A friend asks if you want to get together Friday or Saturday, so you opt in for Friday. She asks if you want Mexican or Japanese. You decide on Mexican to practice asserting your voice.
- Your best friend Ian calls to ask if he can borrow $100. Ian hasn't always been the best at paying you back. You take a breath and say, "My money is all tied up right now." Nothing further. Let Ian have his reaction and the dignity to figure out his own financial jam.

Feel free to prewarn people that you're practicing your *no muscle* and that you're going to be flexing it a lot more. This can offer some humor, provide some clarity, and may decrease the shock value of your new stance.

Extremist

Do you take your *yes* answers to the extreme? Are you a *yes person*? Is it important that people like you? Do you find yourself wanting to please people? Are you the parent who tends to say *yes*? Is it impossible for you to let go of other's disappointment and anger?

Maybe a *yes* hiatus is in your best interest. If so, for the next thirty days, consider saying *no* to every request, no matter how trite.

Think of someone who needs a drastic health intervention. No sugar, no processed foods, and no dairy for thirty days. Seems extreme, but necessary, perhaps. An extreme measure may be exactly what you need to break your *yes* habit. When the time is right to reintroduce *yes,* you can take note of your signs and symptoms to see what your reactions are and where you start to decline.

People I can start saying no to are:	

Things I can start saying no to are:	

Some things others may ask me to do are:	My response will be:

Responding to Urgency

"A lack of planning on your part
does not make for an emergency on my part."
~ Unknown

Nowhere is it written that you must give an immediate response to someone's request. You have every right to take your time in preparing your response. As you establish your footing in the face of conflict, it is helpful to take time to sort through your feelings and best interest.

When was the last time you flew off the handle? One minute you're meandering along, when suddenly, the slightest wrong move sends your heart racing and your blood boiling. Words begin to fly out of your mouth, landing you in full blown rage fest. Meanwhile, those around you don't even know what hit them. Everyone, including you, sits wondering, *what the hell just happened*?

Reactions like these don't come out of thin air. In fact, they tend to stem from layers of built up frustrations and overwhelm. In the face of conflict, clients often say to me, "Oh, I'm okay. I just let that go." Immediately, I stop them to check if a heap of emotions are piled up from everything they've claimed to *let go of*. Some people really are very easy going, but what I find to be truer is that people try to *let go* of the things they are working to avoid, mainly because they don't know how to address it.

There is a vast difference between reacting vs. responding. The difference can completely alter the exchange you have with someone, and certainly, the outcome too.

Reactions tend to be emotionally fueled; driven from the *fight or flight* part of your brain. There's a sense of urgency, hostility, and impulsivity. These responses can be layered with assumptions and false motives. Reactions are not the most effective way for you to approach a situation/problem, gain understanding and connection, or come to a solution.

Responding is more thoughtful because you've taken the time to assess and think through a situation. It is a more deliberate, well-thought-out way to communicate your point. A response stems from the current situation, rather than highly intensified past emotional hurts. Knowing how to respond, rather than react, is vital in communicating effectively.

If something deserves your attention and you're feeling the heat of an emotional reaction, it is perfectly fine to buy some time. Calming yourself down, sorting through your feelings, and thinking about how you really want to handle the situation are all great ways to use logic in navigating emotional situations.

Below are ways to buy some time.

- I'll get back to you.
- I'll call you later.
- I need some time to think about that.
- I'm not sure how I feel about that. I'm going to sit on it for a bit.
- Let me see how I feel that day.
- I'm going to sleep on it.
- I need a day or two to take it all in.
- There are a few questions I have before I decide.
- I'm not ready to talk about this.

- That's interesting. I'll look into it.
- This is a lot to take in. I'll need to process it.
- I want to give this the attention it needs. I'm going to think about it.
- I'm not in the best place to decide right now.
- This stirs up some thoughts and emotions for me, and I want to give you a fair response.

Rather than reacting with a dramatic *no* or from an overly emotional place, you can offer any of the above options to calm down and rationalize. Afterward, you are still entitled to say *no* and are allowed to feel what you are feeling. However, now you're not *driven* from a heated place where you're bound to make a bad situation worse.

When you take your signs of stress and respond respectfully and assertively to them, others begin to take you more seriously. Also, you act in your own best interest without frenzied drama working against you.

Chapter 24

SOS

"I had to stop hoping so much that a ship would rescue me. I should not count on outside help. Survival had to start with me. In my experience, a castaway's worst mistake is to hope too much and to do too little. Survival starts by paying attention to what is close at hand and immediate. To look out with idle hope is tantamount to dreaming one's life away."

~ Yann Martel

Have you ever sent out an S.O.S.? Have you been in such extreme distress that you wanted something or someone to save you?

What if I told you the Morse Code S.O.S. doesn't have a specific meaning? Those letters don't stand for anything. Overtime, because of its use in distress, there's a mistaken belief that S.O.S. means *Save Our Ships* or *Save Our Souls*; but, nope, it doesn't, it holds no meaning at all.

In the most supportive and empowering way, I need to inform you, there is nobody coming to rescue you. No one will swoop in to save your day; no matter how many S.O.S. calls you send, no matter your fairytales, and your romantic dreams. Life offers a universal truth that everyone has lessons to learn and nobody comes through life's portal unscathed. Your healing is up to you.

Knowing your life's restoration is in your hands, how are you navigating the rough waters? When the waves feel like they are crashing in, how will you find solid ground? What if I told you there is another code? A code that includes the same letters, S.O.S.? What if this S.O.S. code unlocks a dynamic toolbox, that in times of insidious distress, can restore you to a calm, serene shore during the storms? Would you use it?

When used correctly, this code will align you with your deepest, most genuine, authentic self. This S.O.S. code reveals your *Sense Of Self,* in which ten powerful tools offer you hope and healing.

Once you reach adulthood, nobody is responsible, nor fully capable, of healing your aches, except you. Your journey is as spiritual as it is emotional and physical. Hopefully you will find the purpose in your pain, while trusting that it is intended for good and growth—not as some cruel punishment by a malicious cosmic creator.

If life's old sanctioned notice and all the unreasonable terms of engagement have damn near killed you, it's time to look within. If the stuff outside of you (people, places, and things) have been your main bag of tricks, you may find they have run their course. If the pieces of your life no longer fit, you can decide how to rebuild and with whom.

You don't have to wait for permission or some golden opportunity to take responsibility for your life. You must become your greatest resource and strongest advocate. You deserve your own love and attention. Utilize your voice to honor your feelings, needs, and desires. Though you may still appreciate the praise and approval of others, you can no longer be driven by it since you will still be actively seeking attention as a way of measuring your worth.

Your previous ways of functioning in the world may have served you and others for a time. You did the best you could with what you had, but now, it's time to function differently. Maya Angelou said, "When you know better, do better." It's time to do better!

Below is a sneak peek into your new toolbox. Each dynamic tool equips and empowers you to reach within as you function in the world from a new, strengthened, self-determined place.

S.O.S.

- Self-Anchoring
- Self-Awareness
- Self-Compassion
- Self-Define
- Self-Honesty
- Self-Honoring

- Self-Permission
- Self-Referencing
- Self-Respect
- Self-Responsibility

Each one of these power tools will help you navigate life much easier. They are incredibly useful in conflict, decision making, relationships, and managing your emotions. They help you become your very best guide and advocate.

Like anything new, these tools may seem confusing and foreign, at first. They may take some practice to implement and may be awkward when you first begin. You can use one tool at a time or several in conjunction with others during more complicated storms. No matter how you decide to use them, remember, you will have them at your fingertips to guide your emotions and decisions.

In the next section of this book, you will learn about each tool in the S.O.S. toolbox in greater depth. Like any other toolbox, you won't use every single one of these tools for every job. You will learn which tool will help you get each unique job done right. Each will help you build a firm foundation from which you can proudly declare your new sanctioned notice and updated terms of engagement. Good luck on your journey of using each tool effectively to build the life you truly deserve.

Inside Your S.O.S. Toolbox

(Use QR Scanner on your cell phone to watch videos.)

www.AllysonBlythe.com

POWER TOOL #1

Self-Anchoring

Are you easily swept up by your emotions or the emotions of others? Do you have a hard time separating how you feel from what others are feeling? Does conflict intimidate and overwhelm you? Do you project the worst-case scenario and head straight for disaster when stress hits? When life catches you off guard and things change, do you have a tough time shifting to Plan B?

If you're not careful, emotions will toss you into treacherous waters, leaving you unable to find your footing and feeling as though you may drown. Like the whirling dangers of a riptide, emotions often overpower logic.

Self-anchoring is the ability to stabilize yourself and gain perspective in stressful or uncertain situations. It is the ability to find your footing in the midst of deep emotion or conflict; to take a deep breath and find some logic and reason to a situation that feels stressful and overwhelming.

Heavy emotions such as fear, worry, or panic may propel you into dark thoughts that exacerbate your emotions further. Thought patterns like blame, assuming, assigning motives, hopelessness, and worst-case scenarios will add much heat to your internal fire. *Self-anchoring* is the ability to recognize these patterns to gain perspective about what you're feeling and what's actually happening in a situation.

When you don't know how to ground yourself, it's easy to get swept up into a situation and get carried away by your emotions. When you're stressed and triggered, *self-anchoring* allows you to reason with your feelings and find the confidence and stability needed to gain an accurate perspective.

Have you ever driven a manual vehicle? How long did it take you to learn to slowly and steadily let off the clutch while giving it gas to switch gears? How many times did you stall out in the middle of an intersection? You probably know you can't go straight from first to fifth gear and have it turn out well.

Learning to shift through your emotions can be very much like shifting gears in a manual car. Recognizing low gear emotions such as fear, despair, rage, and resentment must be processed and worked through before moving into rational, logical gears. Learning to smoothly and gently move through raw emotions is an essential dynamic of *self-anchoring*. *Self-anchoring* is a way to establish firm logical ground where you can respond to a situation, rather than react.

Here's an example:
You walk into the office Friday afternoon and are handed a pink slip. Your immediate response is one of devastation, rage, and failure. You gather your belongings, all while chastising yourself: *This is awful. What are people going to think about me? I'll never recover from this. I am such an idiot for even trying for this job.* Raw, heavy emotion is understandable.

Then as you walk out the door, humbly carrying your box, you begin to angrily question your own feelings: *What is wrong with me? Why am I so pissed off? I've hated that job for years; I should be happy. Why am I such an idiot to even care about this place? I should be relieved, grateful even.*

And therein lies the dilemma. You're facing a really difficult situation that evokes a wide array of deep feelings. That alone can be some profound emotional waters to navigate. Then, you try to force yourself into a logical perspective, judging and shaming your emotions. Those waters can become treacherous if you don't grab your S.O.S. tools.

Self-Anchoring is the ability to recognize and acknowledge your feelings, see the scope of a situation, and then speak logically to yourself without ridicule and judgment.

An example of *self-anchoring* may sound like: *Damn,*

I've hated that job for years, but no one wants to be fired. It sucks that it wasn't my choice, but the severance package gives me more than six months to find something new; or better yet, start working on that business idea I've always had. Maybe, just maybe, this is a blessing in disguise; but right now I'm pretty pissed off.

Another example: You've been in conflict with your mother-in-law for years. When you walk into the family Christmas dinner, she comments on your weight. Your initial thoughts might be: *Maybe I'll pound her with some holiday cheer. You know what? She's right. I am a fat ass. I have been hammering down the holiday cookies every night for a week. Everyone can probably tell. I'm just going to leave now.*

A *self-anchoring* response may look like this: *Ouch! That one hurt. I'm frustrated with myself for the way I've been eating, and I'm embarrassed that she called me out in front of everyone. I didn't deserve that. I know I have some responsibility in this, but I've decided to let myself off the hook during the holidays. I'll get back to it after the first of the year. It's hard when she speaks to me like that.*

Emotions settle when they are acknowledged. Trying to force yourself into fifth-gear logic, without properly shifting through your first-gear emotions, will likely escalate the situation, like trying to swallow something you haven't properly chewed. Denying, suppressing, and minimizing your feelings will only save them for a later date when they ooze out in some other way. Judging, shaming, and ridiculing emotion just further complicates them. The goal is simply to recognize and name the feeling without getting caught up in the added story or trying to shift them too quickly.

Offering someone logic in response to emotional situations, will leave them feeling invalidated, misunderstood, and unsupported. Doing that to yourself is terrible self-betrayal. You can't go wrong with validating an emotion, then, and only then, can you assure them with logic.

What does *self-anchoring* look like?

- Recognize, understand, and soothe your feelings
- Accurately assess a situation and see it in proportion
- Find your footing in the face of turmoil or conflict
- Separate yourself from what others are feeling or experiencing without getting swept up into it
- Trust yourself enough to know what's best
- Have a sense of safety and reliability that you'll act in your own best interest
- Respond with calm and logic, rather than reacting with raw emotion
- Be resilient
- Recoup and recover from difficulty

www.AllysonBlythe.com

POWER TOOL #2

Self-Awareness

Have you ever arrived somewhere, then, in a moment of panic, you realize you have no idea how you got there? You pull into the parking lot and anxiously wonder: *Did I stop at that stop sign? Did I lock the front door? Did I turn off the coffee pot?*

Have your behaviors become so routinely automatic that you are unaware of what you're doing and why you're doing it? Do you do things just because it's what's expected of you, and it's the way it has always been done?

Self-awareness, by far, is one of the most powerful tools you can have. It's the ability to plug in, inform yourself, and pay attention to your thoughts, feelings, and sensations, as well as tuning in to others and your surroundings. *Self-awareness* is also the ability to see where you're going and pay attention to what's happening.

What does *self-awareness* look like?

- Function from a place of consciousness
- Stay awake to what's going on internally and externally
- Tune in to what you think, feel, want, and need
- Eliminate autopilot performances
- Let go of pleasing and performing
- Know your motive behind doing what you're doing
- Consciously use proper words
- Control your thoughts
- Know your personal triggers and what it feels like when they are activated
- Make decisions effectively
- Powerfully solve problems

POWER TOOL #3

Self-Compassion

Have you become your own worst enemy? Are you haunted and taunted by your inner critic? Do you refer to yourself in a demeaning, unkind manner? Would you ever speak to a child the way you speak to yourself?

Your thoughts matter. Your brain will believe whatever you tell it and look for evidence to prove your beliefs. Your words matter just as much as your thoughts. Your words carry energy and highly influence the way you think, feel, and behave, whether you realize it or not.

Your internal and external dialogue creates a lens through which you see yourself, other people, and situations. Negative thoughts carry negative energy, just as positive thoughts carry positive energy. Your thoughts become habitual, automatic, well-trained, and well-rehearsed. Since your brain buys whatever story you sell it, why not change it to a positive, majestic story? Why not celebrate and acknowledge your strengths, assets, achievements, and all that is purely right in the world?

Self-compassion is a great place to start. It is the ability to be kind and understanding toward yourself, even when you make monumental mistakes. It helps you anchor and soothe your strongest emotions. Though your inner critic plays a wise and discerning chief role in your life, it can be destructive when allowed to roam freely, with its sharp edges and unhealed wounds. Allowing your inner critic to rule the roost is like allowing a bully to oversee the playground.

Do you remember the Saturday Night Live skit featuring Stuart Smalley, where he says: "I'm good enough, smart enough, and doggone it, people like me."? It's a comical skit where Stuart, in efforts to boost his self-esteem with encouragement and acknowledgment, speaks those words while looking into a mirror. Though certainly funny, it seemed to make a mockery of self-affirmations and positive self-talk; perhaps setting the tone that you're a wuss if you are encouraging and kind to yourself. Tragic, really.

Yes, self-affirmations and positive self-talk can seem silly and feel ridiculous, at first. Yet the more you practice, the more natural it becomes; and the more your body, brain, and spirit can heal from your past damaging thoughts and words.

What if you became your own soft place to land? What

if you were someone you could always count on? What if you stopped battering yourself, and instead, became genuinely kind and respectful to yourself? What if you committed to meeting your own needs for acknowledgment and appreciation?

Imagine speaking to yourself the way you would speak to a small child; celebrating your strengths and reassuring yourself through difficult situations. Imagine referring to yourself with high regard, respect, and love.

Your words matter, so be willing to speak assuredly to yourself. You can start now by creating a kind nickname for yourself; and if you really want to stretch your comfort zone, practice *mirror work*. You can speak quietly if it makes you more comfortable in the beginning. You may giggle, look away, and have all kinds of uncomfortable thoughts and feelings. Stick with it! It's worth it! You have the power to retrain your brain.

Mirror Work

Mirror work is the process of making eye contact with yourself in the mirror and speaking aloud. Ridiculous as it may feel, it is a powerful tool that allows you to affirm your message. You can tune in to your body language and nonverbals to further empower yourself. Practice your responses repeatedly, matching it with your body language and posture. Sure, it feels silly, but it works!

What does *self-compassion* look like?

- Pay attention to how you talk, think, and act toward yourself
- Monitor your internal script and default belief system when stress hits
- Use kind, gentle, and understanding attitudes, behaviors, and words
- Honor all parts of yourself; even the parts you don't like
- Recognize mistakes and be accountable for them without shame
- Have a spirit of curiosity, seeking to understand, and noticing, rather than judging and ridiculing
- Recognize weakness as something that doesn't work for you, rather than unworthiness *(If you're not good at math, you're not good at math. It doesn't have to mean you're stupid or incapable.)*

POWER TOOL #4

Self-Define

How does your family measure success? What does your religion teach about marriage and the roles of men and women? What defines happiness in your culture? Were family rules and expectations subtle or direct? Do the messages and beliefs you were raised with suit you and your best interest or are they just well-established habits that you learned long ago?

Perhaps you look outside of yourself to discover what you should or shouldn't be doing. Maybe the rules of happiness, love, success, or spirituality have been defined from your family and your background. Making decisions for yourself or having a perspective that's not influenced by all your training may be challenging. Have you forced yourself into a mold that doesn't even fit?

Self-defining is the process of creating an intentional, empowered definition of your life. It is gaining clarity and direction for your life's purpose and accomplishments. It is the ability to decide for yourself what you want and how you want your life to look. *Self-defining* lets you create your own personal vision of major life concepts, such as success, happiness, and love.

Major life issues such as career, relationships, happiness, success, failure, and fun, are defined, role modeled, and reinforced as the way life *should be*. Expectations are established that a successful life should resemble that which your family role modeled.

No one went to college in Andre's family. They seemed destined for poverty. He knew from the time he was little that he was meant for something bigger. Books opened a world far beyond the city limits, and he was ignited to study abroad someday. His family taunted and teased him, interrogating, *who the hell do you think you are?* The college acceptance letters became even more of the fuel he needed to propel him into the life he really wanted to create for himself.

Sonya was 42 years old and never married. She wanted a child more than anything and decided to look into adoption. Her religious family was mortified at the idea and declared their refusal to support her parenting a child outside of traditional marriage. Sonya proceeded with the adoption process and was deeply hurt by her family's decision to sever ties with her.

The morale of *honor thy father and mother* has perhaps

caused more confusion, stress, trauma, and misconstrued loyalty, unlike anything else I've seen. Somehow *honor* has been interpreted as no boundaries, no limits, and blind loyalty beyond what's in your best interest.

Self-defining allows you to rewrite your personal definitions and decide for yourself what you want to create in your life, despite old training and belief structures. It is the ability to look within to see if those well-trained expectations are serving you or if you need to redefine.

There comes a point in life when you can take the wheel and rewrite your script. *Self-defining* allows you to establish personalized views and beliefs that suit your best interest and deepest desires for your life.

What does *self-defining* look like?

- Know who you are and what your purpose is
- Evaluate your own worth and best interest
- Heed your instincts and life calling
- Question the accuracy and effectiveness of what you've been taught
- Align your behavior, decisions, and relationships with what you most desire
- Say *yes* and *no* appropriately
- Realize your personal truth, rather than social and familial training
- Discern what feels good and what doesn't

- Trust your ability to assess situations and decide appropriately
- Use your feelings and gut sense to clarify your preferences and truths

POWER TOOL #5

Self-Honesty

How often do you bullshit yourself? Do you worry about what other people think? Are you involved in relationships, groups, or projects that are not in your best interest? Are you afraid of change? Do you justify, excuse, or minimize things because you're not able to face the truth? Do you pretend and perform?

How does it feel when someone you love lies to you? Most likely, it is a devastating blow that is hard to recover from. It's almost as shattering as realizing you've been lying to yourself about something.

Self-honesty is the ability to tell yourself the full truth about what is happening in your life. Justifying, minimizing, excusing, and blaming are all indicators that you're not being honest with yourself.

Conflict can be scary; so instead of being honest, many

people minimize, justify, or excuse things in order to avoid truth. Facing the reality of certain situations forces you to look at difficult facts and come to terms with tougher decisions needing to be made.

Imagine eating a shit sandwich and pretending you like it. Every bite forces you to muster the strength and determination to sink your teeth into it. It's disgusting, you know this and everyone else knows it; yet there you are, bellied up to the table diving in. Why not just acknowledge the truth and deal with it accordingly?

Have you been eating your own dose of shit sandwiches? Are you denying or justifying things in your life? Are you ready to deal with the stuff you don't like?

Understand, not being ready to take action is different than lying to yourself. If you're not ready, you can still tell yourself the truth about the situation. Maybe you're in a relationship that is really bad for you, but the sex is good, and you just don't want to end it, yet. Perhaps you have a toxic friend, but the length of the friendship trumps the quality of it. Maybe you hate your job, but are afraid to start over, so you try to stay focused on its benefits and flexibility.

You're an adult. You get to decide what you tolerate and what you don't; what you're ready to change and what you aren't. Either way, it's important to tell yourself the truth to honor what's really happening.

Though people mistake the two, acceptance is much

different from approval. Acceptance is seeing the reality of the situation; the acknowledgment that *it is what it is.* Approval is liking something or seeing it as good. You may need to accept that it is raining on your parade. Acceptance allows you to adjust the situation as it is, rather than how you wish it were. *Self-honesty* allows you to accept a situation, no matter how difficult it may be.

Whether it's love, friendship, work, or something else, if the relationship doesn't suit you, at some point, you must stop living a fictitious romance novel, naively hoping it will magically get better or fix itself. (Stop eating the proverbial shit sandwich.) Anything you excuse, minimize, pretend, or justify is probably an example of a shit sandwich that you're trying to swallow.

Are you ready to acknowledge the things that need your attention? Are you ready to stop making excuses that keep you trapped in a life you don't even want? These truths you discover may be ugly, but they are your truth and they deserve your honesty and attention.

What does *self-honesty* look like?

- End the bullshit story and acknowledge the truth
- Practice acceptance without mistaking it as approval

- Tell yourself the truth without pretending, pleasing, blaming, justifying, dressing it up, calling it something else, minimizing, denying, fantasizing, excusing, or getting swept up in the story
- Know thy self: your patterns, wounds, excuses, fears, and triggers; manage these lovingly and effectively
- Be genuine and authentic
- Let your walls down
- Manage vulnerability
- Be open to constructive input and feedback
- Explain without justifying yourself
- Acknowledge how you feel
- Recognize and assert your needs
- Admit when you make a mistake, and learn from them
- See things from an honest, right sized perspective without shrinkage or exaggeration
- Tell the truth even if it upsets someone or has a negative consequence

POWER TOOL #6

Self-Honoring

Does your behavior match what you want in life? Are you disrespecting your body, mind, spirit, or space? Are you allowing others to disrespect your body, mind, spirit, or space? Are you compromising your own value? Are you accommodating to those who don't recognize your worth? Do you play small so others remain comfortable? Do you keep yourself safe within the confines of your comfort zone?

This is where the rubber meets the road. It's one thing to know and understand yourself; it's another to begin to act upon, protect, and honor those things.

Self-honoring is about aligning your words, behavior, and decisions with what you truly desire. It's making decisions about what you're going to tolerate from yourself and others, what you define is in your best interest, and then acting upon those. It's navigating decisions, relationships, conflicts, and conversations to advocate what's in your best interest, even when others disagree or get upset.

What does *self-honoring* look like?

- Have high self-respect and self-esteem
- Prioritize yourself
- Advocate your best interest, even when it means people will disagree, be upset, or even leave
- Align your words, behaviors, and actions with your truth
- Listen to your inner G.P.S.: Gut, Perception, Sense
- Do what is the most loving thing for yourself
- Embrace and function from your strengths
- Honor difficult truths and be willing to address them
- Stand alone, when necessary
- Function with pride; without apology, shame, or guilt

POWER TOOL #7

Self-Permission

Do you hold yourself back? Are you getting in your own way? Do you make things more difficult than they need to be with overthinking or overcomplicating? Does fear rule most of your decisions? Do you play small to stay safe?

My client, Sally, was a 59-year-old woman struggling with the effects of aging and the toll that years seem to take on a woman's body. Her inner critic tore at her self-esteem daily, creating distance and insecurity in her marriage of over 40 years.

I was curious when she hurriedly came into my office and handed me an envelope, inquiring with only a questioning brow and eyes. She responded, "I did it. I finally did it. I have always wanted to get those pictures done; you know, those sexy ones where you dress up and they do a photoshoot."

"You mean a boudoir session?" I clarified.

"Yes, that's it." She continued, "I've hated my body for more than fifty years, almost my entire life. I've given birth to four children and my husband has been there every step of the way; but I still hide in the closet every time I change my clothes. Finally…," her words choked under the weight of her tears and years of anguish and loathing.

"Finally, I worked up the courage to make the phone call. I've held myself back all these years, but not anymore. Those are the pictures I'm giving to my husband tonight."

Her nervous delight was evident from across the room. Sally had written her own permission slip to do something for herself and her husband—something that honored her body and a secret, playful desire she had always had. She had finally let go of the shame, fear, worry, and insecurities, and simply allowed herself to have fun.

Self-permission is granting yourself a big, fat "YES!" to what you want most in life. It's going after the job, writing the book, taking the trip, asking the question, and stepping fully into the game of life. *Self-permission* is getting out of your own way by letting go of old fears, limitations, and stories. It's taking risks, no matter how big or small.

What does *self-permission* look like?

- Grant yourself permission to say, do, and be who you want
- Let go of excuses
- Walk through the discomfort and fear of trying something new, making mistakes, and looking silly; be proud of yourself for trying
- Live fully without playing small
- Allow yourself to be whoever you're meant to be and to allow others to do the same
- A playful, curious spirit
- Rest when needed
- Decide for yourself
- Stay the course, when you need to, and grant yourself the flexibility to change your mind when necessary

www.AllysonBlythe.com

POWER TOOL #8

Self-Referencing

Do you struggle to make your own decisions? Do you survey others for their opinions about your life? Are you indecisive? Are you easily overwhelmed by choices? Do you try to please or perfect everything? Are you worried that you'll make mistakes?

I can hear Joe Cocker belting it out...

> *"What do I do when my love is away? Does it worry you to be alone? How do I feel at the end of the day? Are you sad because you're on your own? No, I get by with a little help from my friends. Mmm, I get high with a little help from my friends. Mmm, gonna try with a little help from my friends."*

There's nothing wrong with getting support when you need it. Furthermore, there's nothing wrong with asking someone you trust for their opinion when you need to weigh your options. However, this can become a dangerous habit causing you to lose touch with your intuition. Be mindful not to rely heavily on the input and opinions of others.

If you're looking outside of yourself for clarity, direction, and answers, it may be time to begin *self-referencing*. If you're looking to others to decide what you should be doing, thinking, and feeling, it is definitely time to *self-reference*. Make certain you don't allow other people's opinions to smother your voice and truth.

As you navigate life, make your own decisions and feel confident in your knowledge, abilities, and skills. You don't have to know everything; but trusting your *figure-it-out abilities and skills* provides powerful assurance. Knowing when to seek input, and from whom to seek it, are also essential skills.

What does *self-referencing* look like?

- Recognize yourself as your most valuable resource
- Be your strongest advocate
- Trust yourself enough to act in your best interest
- Make decisions that align with who you are
- Increase your reliability and assurance that you can handle life

- Trust your problem-solving skills and know when to ask for input
- Decide what you want and need
- Trust your gut
- Align yourself with your values
- Do what brings you joy, regardless of what other's think
- Honor your "yes"
- Say "no" when necessary
- Know when to *redecide*
- Allow people to feel however they may, regarding your decisions
- Eliminate patterns of pleasing and approval seeking
- Conduct an inner investigation by asking yourself:
    - "What do I think about this?"
    - "How does this feel?"
    - "What would I love right now?"

www.AllysonBlythe.com

POWER TOOL #9

Self-Respect

How well do you treat yourself? Are you removing people, places, and things from your life that don't honor your worth? Are you proud of who you are? Are you confident in your abilities? Do you conduct yourself in ways that command the respect and decency you deserve?

R-E-S-P-E-C-T. Find out what it means to me... My toes can't help but tap when I think about Aretha belting out the power of that tune.

What does respect look like to you? What does respect feel like to you? What are your personal terms and conditions for being treated respectfully? Are you holding yourself and others to those standards?

Every day, and in many ways, you inform people how to treat you and the things you will accept and tolerate. Your words may say one thing, but the evidence is in the language, behavior, posture, and decisions you choose.

If you want to fly your freak flag, by all means, fly away! If certain behaviors, decisions, and relationships enhance your best self, you are free to do whatever you want to do. However, if something is compromising to you, outside of your safety zone, or a desperate attempt to gain attention and approval, you are acting against yourself; ultimately, selling yourself out.

The way you act and speak are invisible radars attracting the people, circumstances, and things you believe you deserve. Disrespecting yourself or tolerating disrespect from others sends a clear message that you don't value yourself. When you compromise yourself, reference yourself negatively, or excuse unacceptable behaviors, you indicate that people can misbehave in your world, and you'll put up with it. Others know you won't do anything about their inappropriate behavior and their level of respect for you plummets.

Like a police officer who repeatedly warns, but never writes the ticket, words without action or consequences are just annoying rambles. They are sounds that people learn to ignore. It will always be up to you to define how others are allowed to treat you.

What does *self-respect* look like?

- Function from a place of personal dignity and integrity

- Use behaviors, words, and thoughts that honor who you are and how you want to be treated
- Align your behavior with your morals, ethics, and values
- Have standards and boundaries
- Be assertive, clear, and respectful to yourself and others
- Honor your body with how you allow yourself to be treated and spoken to
- Be mindful of the things you accept, tolerate, and laugh at
- Use respectful and honoring language toward yourself (Don't call yourself names.)
- Use loving and respectful behaviors
- Make honorable decisions

www.AllysonBlythe.com

www.AllysonBlythe.com

POWER TOOL #10

Self-Responsibility

Are you waiting for prince/princess charming? Are you hoping that someday, somehow, someone will come rescue you? Do you blame others for your struggles and passively wait for someone or something to fix it? Are you often the victim? Is it hard for you to make choices for yourself? Are you waiting for someone's permission or approval in life?

It is a momentous day when you realize your life is fully up to you. No one is waiting in the wings to fix, heal, or rescue you. If things are going to change, it's up to you to align with people, places, and things that help you be your best self. It's up to you to eliminate anything that gets in the way of your best possible life.

Yes, some terrible shit may have gone down in your life, and some people have treated you terribly. There's no denying that happens in life. It's important to acknowledge it, grieve, heal, and move passed it into a place of responsibility. Though you may not be to blame for some things, you are now responsible for your own healing. In some parts, you may have even played a role that you'll want to look at. There comes a point when you must take control of your healing and begin the next part of your journey.

What does *self-responsibility* look like?

- Take full responsibility for your life
- Evaluate your options, even if they're difficult or awful
- Be honest about your role in the details, no matter how big or small
- Take responsibility for your role in the matter
- Make decisions that honor what's in your best interest
- Manage conflict directly and respectfully
- Acknowledge and soothe your challenging emotions
- Detach from others
- Be self-reliant
- Mobilize your efforts for what you want and need, rather than waiting on others
- Hit the reset button on your thoughts, feelings, actions, and attitude
- Prioritize self-care: boundaries, rest, appointments, nurturance, and play

There you have it! Ten simple, incredibly dynamic tools that will help change the course of your life. Ten tools that will empower you and help you step into your fullest sense of self and achieve the life you've always deserved.

www.AllysonBlythe.com

Final Thoughts

Claiming Your Well-Being

Congratulations! You've stuck with it! Job well done, my friend! Do you see evidence of your well-spent commodities? Are your relationships starting to shift? Are they shifting for better, or for worse?

Keep going. I promise you, there is another side to this. Take note of your progress and be willing to be your best guide and advocate. Hold gentle, compassionate space for your struggles and losses. Your journey deserves to be honored, celebrated, and grieved.

Remember, old patterns can take time to lessen their grip. The more you practice, the more successful you will be. Before you know it, new, healthy patterns will form. Retraining your brain is the same as reconditioning your body. It takes daily focus and discipline as you keep your eyes on the prize. There is no greater prize than living the life you were meant to live. Train your brain and your heart to act in your best interest.

Find a success partner. Who in your life is able and willing to walk this path with you? Is there a friend who can also benefit from some boundary work? Is there someone you know who has strong boundary setting skills and who can serve as a role model?

I encourage you to hire someone to guide you on your road to success; someone who will cheer for you, challenge you, and celebrate with you every step of the way.

Putting pen to paper about what you want will propel you to new levels of clarity and success. Don't just think about it, write it down. If you have a win, document it. If you find yourself in a difficult situation, process it with your words. Writing about your journey will help you travel the path, honor the details, and give you a different perspective, rather than having your thoughts bounce off the same old four corners of your mind.

Typically, people quit or never even start to change because of fear and uncertainty. The unfamiliar is one of the scariest places you have never visited. Perhaps you've designed most of your life around avoiding these places. Do your best to normalize your fears and use them as evidence that you're doing the right thing. Managing your fears and uncertainties will help you navigate and solidify the S.O.S. tools.

I wish you all the best on your continued journey into kindness, authenticity, and no longer being misunderstood.

~ Allyson Blythe

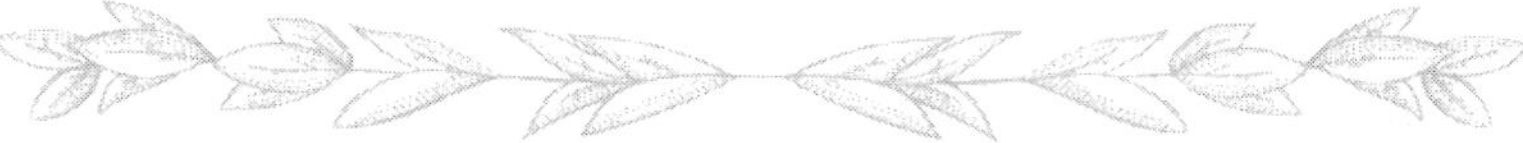

What's Next?

Since starting my career more than twenty-five years ago, I have worked with thousands of people in a variety of settings. Even more, I have developed a community of like-minded people who are dedicated to their journey of success.

My commitment lies within traveling with those I work with on their personal path of transformation. My clients are educated on their patterns, thoughts, habits, hidden stories, and beliefs that get in their way. Then, they are equipped with powerful tools and resources to propel them to new levels of awareness, courage, and success. Finally, they are empowered through support, connection, and accountability as we walk together creating the life they've always wanted.

The clients I work with are ready—ready to let go of their old patterns, fear, worry, and playing small. They are ready for a no-nonsense approach of stepping into the game of life and giving it their best shot, once and for all. I am honored to offer a wide range of opportunities to support them, and you, along the way:

- Individual Coaching Sessions
- Group Life Coaching Courses:
    - B.A.L.A.N.C.E.
    - Radical Self-Care
    - Dedicated Life Overhaul

www.AllysonBlythe.com

- C.B.D.: Commodities, Boundaries, Decision Making
- Online Workshop: The Art of Effective Communication

When you're ready to finally let go of your fear, old patterns, and obstacles, and are ready to step into your full purpose, I would be honored to work with you. Be sure to connect with me at:

www.AllysonBlythe.com

AllysonBlythe@live.com

859-341-7773

Don't wait! Now is your time to shine! Come join our community and let's celebrate all that life has to offer you.

About The Author

Allyson Blythe opened her private practice in 2000 as a Certified Life Coach and LCSW. Raised in Upstate NY, Allyson earned her master's degree from Syracuse University as a social worker and later became a Licensed Clinical Social Worker (LCSW). Allyson educates, equips, and empowers others to dig deep into self-awareness, emotional intelligence, and personal responsibility. Her end goal for her clients is for them to live their very best life.

Allyson states, "I love what I do. This work is much more than a *job*. It's a soul journey that I'm blessed to walk through with my clients."

She strongly believes in meeting her clients where they are with honesty and authenticity. She offers acknowledgment and acceptance to empower her clients to raise the bar on their thoughts and behaviors. This way, they can finally let go of fear, excuses, and old habits to reach their ultimate goals.

With over twenty-five years in the field, Allyson has earned her reputation as a trusted, deeply experienced, and highly intuitive Therapist and Coach.

Allyson invests in her clients' well-being by supporting,

challenging, and guiding them along their journey. She challenges them to go beyond their comfort zone as they stretch and grow.

Those who work with her report real results and lasting change in new levels of self-worth, relationship health, communication, self-understanding, personal performance, and overall mood and functioning.

Regardless of her clients' paths, she comes alongside of them to help them develop their strengths, celebrate their successes, and reach their greatest potential.

In addition to her private practice, Allyson offers seminars, workshops, group coaching, and education from the stage as a Public Speaker. Her content ranges from powerful and dynamic self-discovery workshops to year long coaching programs to help her clients create the life they dream.

Her most popular workshop is *The Art of Effective Communication* where she has helped thousands understand themselves and communicate with others. Allyson states, "Group coaching and workshops are one of the most powerful and cost-effective ways for others to create change and reach goals."

Moving to Northern Kentucky in 1997, Allyson resides in Union, Kentucky, a progressive city known for being surrounded by cities with unique, humorous names, such as Big Bone Lick and Sugar Tit. Allyson has one